3x12|05

THE WAY PEOPLE LIVE

Life on an African Slave Ship

Titles in The Way People Live series include:

THE WAY PEOPLE LIVE

Life on an African Slave Ship

by Joseph Kleinman and Eileen Kurtis-Kleinman

Lucent Books, P.O. Box 289011, San Diego, CA 92198-9011

Acknowledgements
Joseph Kleinman and Eileen Kurtis-Kleinman wish to thank the following people for their invaluable help: Captain Michael Anapol, Norman Brouwer, librarian at the South Street Seaport Museum library, and Deborah A. Wright, Reference Archivist at the Avery Research Center for African American History and Culture.

Library of Congress Cataloging-in-Publication Data

Kleinman, Joseph, 1948-
  Life on an African slave ship / by Joseph Kleinman and Eileen Kurtis-Kleinman.
      p. cm. — (The way people live)
Includes bibliographical references and index.
  ISBN 1-56006-653-9 (alk. paper)
  1. Slave Trade—Africa—History—Juvenile literature. [1. Slave trade—Africa. 2. Slavery. 3. Afro-Americans—History.] I. Kurtis-Kleinman, Eileen.
II. Title. III. Series
  HT1321 .K54 2001
  380.1'44'096—dc21

                                      00-009631
                                         CIP
                                         AC

Contents

Discovering the Humanity in Us All

Books in The Way People Live series focus on groups of people in a wide variety of circumstances, settings, and time periods. Some books focus on different cultural groups, others, on people in a particular historical time period, while others cover people involved in a specific event. Each book emphasizes the daily routines, personal and historical struggles, and achievements of people from all walks of life.

To really understand any culture, it is necessary to strip the mind of the common notions we hold about groups of people. These stereotypes are the archenemies of learning. It does not even matter whether the stereotypes are positive or negative; they are confining and tight. Removing them is a challenge that's not easily met, as anyone who has ever tried it will admit. Ideas that do not fit into the templates we create are unwelcome visitors—ones we would prefer remain quietly in a corner or forgotten room.

The cowboy of the Old West is a good example of such confining roles. The cowboy was courageous, yet soft-spoken. His time (it is always a he, in our template) was spent alternatively saving a rancher's daughter from certain death on a runaway stagecoach, or shooting it out with rustlers. At times, of course, he was likely to get a little crazy in town after a trail drive, but for the most part, he was the epitome of inner strength. It is disconcerting to find out that the cowboy is human, even a bit childish. Can it really be true that cowboys would line up to help the cook on the trail drive grind coffee, just hoping he would give them a little stick of peppermint candy that came with the coffee shipment? The idea of tough cowboys vying with one another to help "Coosie" (as they called their cooks) for a bit of candy seems silly and out of place.

So is the vision of Eskimos playing video games and watching MTV, living in prefab housing in the Arctic. It just does not fit with what "Eskimo" means. We are far more comfortable with snow igloos and whale blubber, harpoons and kayaks.

Although the cultures dealt with in Lucent's The Way People Live series are often historically and socially well known, the emphasis is on the personal aspects of life. Groups of people, while unquestionably affected by their politics and their governmental structures, are more than those institutions. How do people in a particular time and place educate their children? What do they eat? And how do they build their houses? What kinds of work do they do? What kinds of games do they enjoy? The answers to these questions bring these cultures to life. People's lives are revealed in the particulars and only by knowing the particulars can we understand these cultures' will to survive and their moments of weakness and greatness.

This is not to say that understanding politics does not help to understand a culture. There is no question that the Warsaw ghetto, for example, was a culture that was brought about by the politics and social ideas of Adolf

Hitler and the Third Reich. But the Jews who were crowded together in the ghetto cannot be understood by the Reich's politics. Their life was a day-to-day battle for existence, and the creativity and methods they used to prolong their lives is a vital story of human perseverance that would be denied by focusing only on the institutions of Hitler's Germany. Knowing that children as young as five or six outwitted Nazi guards on a daily basis, that Jewish policemen helped the Germans control the ghetto, that children attended secret schools in the ghetto and even earned diplomas—these are the things that reveal the fabric of life, that can inspire, intrigue, and amaze.

Books in The Way People Live series allow both the casual reader and the student to see humans as victims, heroes, and onlookers. And although humans act in ways that can fill us with feelings of sorrow and revulsion, it is important to remember that "hero," "predator," and "victim" are dangerous terms. Heaping undue pity or praise on people reduces them to objects, and strips them of their humanity.

Seeing the Jews of Warsaw only as victims is to deny their humanity. Seeing them only as they appear in surviving photos, staring at the camera with infinite sadness, is limiting, both to them and to those who want to understand them. To an object of pity, the only appropriate response becomes "Those poor creatures!" and that reduces both the quality of their struggle and the depth of their despair. No one is served by such two-dimensional views of people and their cultures.

With this in mind, The Way People Live series strives to flesh out the traditional, two-dimensional views of people in various cultures and historical circumstances. Using a wide variety of primary quotations—the words not only of the politicians and government leaders, but of the real people whose lives are being examined—each book in the series attempts to show an honest and complete picture of a culture removed from our own by time or space.

By examining cultures in this way, the reader will notice not only the glaring differences from his or her own culture, but also will be struck by the similarities. For indeed, people share common needs—warmth, good company, stability, and affirmation from others. Ultimately, seeing how people really live, or have lived, can only enrich our understanding of ourselves.

Voyage of Cruelty

Growth of the New World depended on African slave labor. Slaves tilled the land in North America and the West Indies and mined precious ores in South America, bringing wealth to the European settlers. Transporting these slaves across the Atlantic became a key concern. Between the sixteenth and nineteenth centuries, the most efficient way to carry people and goods from Africa to the Americas was by boat. During this three-hundred-year period, millions of Africans crossed the Atlantic in ships originally intended to carry cargo.

Most historians agree that, for the Africans, life aboard these ships was brutal and inhumane. "In the dank, crowded hold, which was about five feet high, the captives were confined in a prone position, occupying no more space than a coffin,"[1] recounts historian John Henrik Clarke.

Many people died during the voyage, the victims of terrible mistreatment. They were whipped, force fed, stowed in crowded slave decks, and frightened into submission. Thomas Trotter, the surgeon aboard the *Brookes,* reported that the slaves were so crammed that they had no room to turn their bodies from one side to the other. One sailor aboard a slaver attested, "I have heard [the slaves] frequently complaining of heat [in the hold], and have seen them fainting, almost dying from want of water."[2] James Morley told the House of Commons that he witnessed sailors forcing bread down the throats of sick and vomiting slaves. "[Then the sailors would] throw medicine over them so that not half went into their mouths—the poor fellows wallowing in their [own] blood . . . and this with blows [from] the cat [a whip called the cat-o'-nine tails]."[3]

A diagram shows slaves packed tightly into the ship's hold, barely having enough room to move.

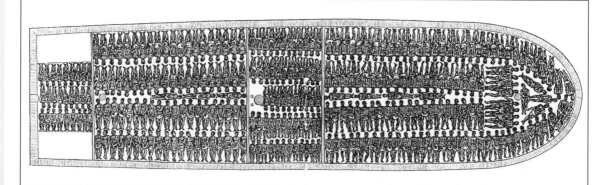

Slave traders usually used a two-hundred-ton, three-masted brig to haul their human cargo.

Slavers often mistreated and brutalized slaves to intimidate them and thereby suppress rebellion. Captain Thomas Phillips of the *Hannibal*, which sailed in 1694, remarked, "I have been informed that some commanders have cut off the legs or arms of the most wilful [slaves], to terrify the rest [and] I was advised by some of my officers to do the same."[4]

Everyday life aboard a slave ship became an unending series of terrible hardships. "To endure the [crossing] required great physical strength, mental toughness, and spiritual resolve,"[5] writes historian Clarke. Torn from their native Africa, slaves were forced to live for weeks or months jammed into an airless, disease-ridden, stinking space below deck. Yet Africans braved this ordeal, often spend-

ing endless days at sea "shackled," as Clarke describes, "two by two, the right wrist and ankle of one to the left wrist and ankle of another."[6] Once ashore, the captives faced new horrors as they were thrust into the slave markets of the New World.

In addition to the plight of the slave, life aboard an African slave ship revolved around the complex working of a two hundred-ton, three-masted brig, the vessel slavers often used. Operating a trading vessel required skills that at the time were considered extremely technologically advanced. During a transatlantic voyage, knowing how to navigate and sail became a matter of survival, around which life aboard all trading ships revolved.

The relationship between slaves and crew was another central part of life at sea. Abused by senior officers and abusive to captives, says Clarke, crew members were "lucky to survive one voyage, and rarely made a second."[7] Seamen aboard slavers also died from the tropical diseases that bred along the African coast and suffered from epidemics that afflicted everyone crowded on the filthy slave ship.

Slave ship captains were often known to mercilessly starve and flog their crew members. The memoirs of the surgeon Alexander Falconbridge record the misdeeds of Captain M'Taggart, but they typify the daily cruelties inflicted by countless other nameless captains. One man, reports Falconbridge, was flogged every day—for no apparent reason—until he jumped overboard into shark-infested waters. The cook aboard the same ship received so severe a beating that he had wounds from his neck to the small of his back. The sadistic captain then dabbed the cook's open cuts with saltwater and cayenne pepper to make the unfortunate seaman writhe in pain. Historians Daniel P. Mannix and Malcom Crowley paint a vivid picture of these men: "They could be seen in Liverpool taverns or haunting the wharves of Charleston . . . men with yellow eyeballs, cheeks sunken with fever, and backs, scarred by the cat; men left behind by their ships and begging for food; men crippled by scurvy."[8]

Brutally mistreated, the crew mistreated the captives as well. The nature of their work, enslaving human beings, required that they harden themselves against any feelings of decency they might have toward their fellow man. As Clarke remarks, "The conditions of [the crew members'] employment forced them to deny the humanity of the Africans; and all too often they began to question the value of their own humanity."[9]

Against these unimaginable odds, treated as less than human, Africans managed to endure the journey. As Clarke observes, "Despite the miserable conditions, inadequate space and food, deadly diseases, and the violence from crew members, millions of African captives survived."[10] Their ability to withstand the harshness of their captors is a testament to their spirit, dignity, and stamina. Clarke describes this quality as an "implacable will"[11] to overcome the hardships aboard the slave ship and to adapt to their life in the New World.

The History of the Slave Trade

In 1746 Olaudah Equiano was eleven years old and lived in the Nigerian village of Isseke as part of the Ibo tribe. He was the youngest son in a well-to-do family and was his mother's favorite. "I was trained up from my earliest years in the art of war," Equiano later wrote in his memoir. "My daily exercise was shooting and throwing javelins, and my mother adorned me with emblems, after the manner of our greatest warriors."[12]

As in most villages in the area, fear of slavers threatened everyone's sense of security. While parents were out working in the fields, slavers used the unguarded moments to seize children and carry them off. Olaudah Equiano was one of those children. As he recalls,

> One day when all our people were gone out to their works as usual, and only I and my dear sister were left to mind the house, two men and a woman got over our walls, and in a moment seized us both, and, without giving us time to cry out, or make resistance, they stopped our mouths, and ran off with us into the nearest woods.[13]

Equianos' was sold more than once, and he traveled from master to master until he found himself on the coast, probably in a port city on the Gulf of Benin. It was the first time he had seen the ocean:

> The first object which saluted my eyes when I arrived on the coast, was the sea, and a slave ship, which was then riding at anchor, and waiting for its cargo. These filled me with astonishment, which was soon converted into terror, when I was carried on board. I was immediately handled, and tossed up to see if I were sound, by some of the crew; and I was now persuaded that I had gotten into a world of bad spirits, and that they were going to kill me. Their complexions, too, differing so much from ours, their long hair, and the language they spoke (which was very different from any I had ever heard), united to confirm me in this belief.[14]

Equiano was not alone. According to historian Robert J. Allison, Equiano was one of fifty thousand Africans taken to the New World that year. By the 1750s slave trading was a highly organized system. African kings, queens, warriors, and farmers from Gambia to Cabinda joined Equiano in his captivity. Over the next hundred years more than 6 million captives suffered the miserable march to the seacoast, where slavers boarded them onto slave ships bound for the New World.

How It Began

The transatlantic slave trade began with a few Portuguese ships in the 1400s, but the practice of slavery had existed for thousands of

Why Africans?

Choosing Africans as the source of slave labor in the New World was a decision Europeans came to over time. At first they tried to enslave the people native to the New World. The Indians of North and South America proved unable to withstand the brutality of slave life or the deadly diseases that Europeans brought with them. "They are not people suited to hard work," wrote Michele Cuneo in the fifteenth century, as quoted by historian Hugh Thomas in *The Slave Trade*. "They suffer from the cold, and they do not have a long life."

Next, the Europeans tried to use indentured servants from Europe. They, too, proved vulnerable to tropical diseases such as malaria. Also, whenever the poor found work in Europe, they were unwilling to leave their homes. In addition, they could run away and hide easily; their skin color allowed them to blend in with free white society.

Europeans turned to Africans as their next alternative. The slave trading system that had existed in Africa for centuries made it easy for Europeans to buy Africans. Once in America, the darker skin color of African slaves made it difficult for these captives to blend in with European society and escape. Finally, some historians assert that prejudiced, greedy Europeans thought that Africans were savage and less than human and viewed these enslaved Africans as domesticated animals.

years. In ancient Egypt, for example, slaves built pyramids for the pharaohs, and in ancient Rome, slaves paved roads. Slavery had long existed in Africa as well, although most slaves there were either prisoners of war or criminals whose punishment included the loss of their freedom. By the time the first Portuguese ships arrived on the African coast in the mid-fifteenth century, the slave market within Africa was well developed. Remarked slave trader Theodore Canot years later, "The financial genius of Africa, instead of devising ban-notes or precious metals as a circulating medium, has from time immemorial declared that a human creature . . . is the most valuable article on earth."[15]

Those Portuguese sailors did not actually travel to Africa in search of slaves. Rather, they hoped to find ivory, spices, and gold. However, in 1441, on his return from a trading expedition in Africa, the Portuguese sailor Atam Goncalvez brought back eight African captives. The captives were presented as a gift to Prince Henry the Navigator, the royal sponsor of Goncalvez's trip.

Unlike their successors, these captives were not mistreated or used for backbreaking physical labor. Rather, they were viewed as oddities and were absorbed into court society. A few years later, in 1481, the slave trade had grown to such a degree that the Portuguese built Elmina, their first slave fort, or barracoon. At Elmina, the Portuguese imprisoned captive Africans before traders loaded them on slave ships.

By the mid-1500s, two hundred years before Olaudah Equiano was kidnapped and forced into slavery, the Portuguese and Spanish began shipping Africans to Europe and to colonies in the Americas. This time, their purpose was to use the captive Africans as slaves.

The colonies were the heart of the slave trade because, as historian John Hope Franklin observes, "there was never any profitable future for African slavery in Europe." The way Europe was developing at that time did not require a vast influx of human labor, and poor Europeans vied for any employment opportunities available. As Europeans searched for new trade routes, new lands, and new commodities to trade, the slave trade grew. "It was the New World," explains Franklin, "with its vast natural resources and its undeveloped regions that could make slavery and the slave trade profitable"[16] for the Europeans.

Expanding to the New World

The drive among Europeans to explore other parts of the world, and their eventual discovery of the New World, began with a reorganization of power. During the Middle Ages, the church held a great deal of power. By the end of the fifteenth century, however, power shifted to the hands of monarchs, and European governments began to form strong nation-states.

These kings and queens were interested in expanding their territories, and they used war and trade to do so. The cost of administering monarchies, establishing government-sponsored commercial trade, and waging war on rival nations often increased government debt. "Diminishing surpluses drove the Europeans to seek resources abroad," says anthropologist Eric R. Wolf, "especially as increased wealth was required to finance the emergent states."[17]

Christopher Columbus lands in the Caribbean in 1492. Columbus's voyage marked the beginning of European expansion into the New World.

This desire to increase wealth spurred Queen Isabella and King Ferdinand of Spain, for example, to sponsor Christopher Columbus's journey across the Atlantic Ocean in 1492. Instead of finding a direct route to India as he had hoped, Columbus sailed to the Caribbean Island known today as Hispaniola and set in motion the direction of Spanish, as well as European, expansion over the next two hundred years.

As historian James Pope-Hennessey contends,

> While the year 1441 may be taken as marking the beginning of the slave trade, the most significant year in its history was 1492, when Christopher Columbus discovered the new World. For the next three and a half centuries and at ever-increasing momentum, the development of the new territories across the Atlantic demanded millions upon millions of African slaves.[18]

When Europeans first settled in the New World, they did not intend to create a slave-based economy. Neither did they imagine building a social structure that included slaves as part of its foundation. According to historian Donald R. Wright, "When the first English colonists settled in Jamestown in 1607, they did not have in mind establishing an economy and society based on slavery." It developed slowly, he says, in part because "colonists with bountiful land were having difficulty finding an adequate, stable labor force to make their [farming] efforts . . . pay."[19]

European colonists quickly discovered that certain areas of the New World were suitable for growing crops that they could sell easily in the European marketplace. For example, sugar and cocoa were products colonists could produce easily in tropical parts of the New World, such as the West Indies and Brazil. Europeans had always relished these two items, but until their cultivation in the New World, sugar and cocoa had been considered rare luxuries, available at a considerable cost to only a privileged few.

According to historian Hugh Thomas, "In 1750, already, 'the poorest English farm labourer's wife took sugar in her tea.'" Furthermore, in 1747 England's best-selling first cookbook included a cake recipe calling for "three quarters of a pound of the best moist sugar."[20]

But, growing sugarcane and mining other resources required a substantial number of workers. In addition, these workers needed to be able to withstand hard labor and extreme heat over a long period. Equally important to European colonists was that the labor cost very little.

African slave labor quickly became the solution. By the beginning of the 1600s, Europeans were focusing on developing a structured slave trading system in Africa. Many Africans willingly took part in this system; African kings routinely met with traders and exchanged slaves for European goods. There were others, however, who protested vehemently against the practice.

In 1526, for instance, the African king Afonso I tried unsuccessfully to ban the slave trade from the Congo. Portuguese traders were destroying his kingdom, and he agonized that "every day people are enslaved and kidnapped, even nobles, even members of the king's own family."[21]

A hundred years later, Queen Nzinga Nbande of Angola attempted to unite several African states against European slave trading. Her efforts failed, but she also organized raiding parties to free captives aboard African slave ships and was known to harbor runaway

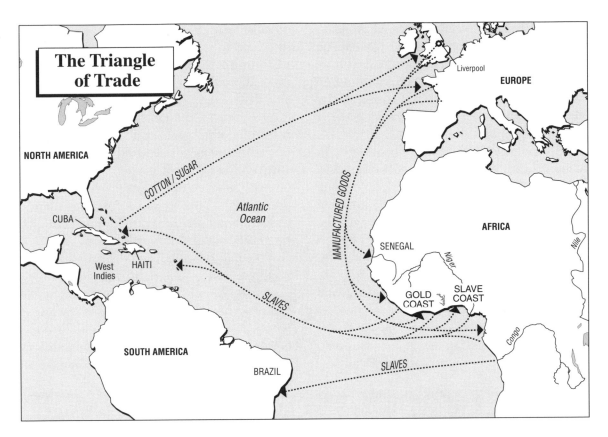

The Triangle of Trade

NORTH AMERICA

COTTON / SUGAR

Atlantic
Ocean

CUBA

West
Indies

HAITI

SLAVES

SOUTH AMERICA

BRAZIL

SLAVES

MANUFACTURED GOODS

Liverpool

EUROPE

AFRICA

SENEGAL

Niger

Nile

GOLD
COAST

SLAVE
COAST

Congo

slaves. Despite these efforts, however, the slave trade continued.

The Triangle of Trade

The Atlantic slave trade was part of the larger transatlantic trading system. This exchange of goods and slaves across the Atlantic Ocean among three or four continents was known as the Triangle of Trade. The name originated from the triangular sea route that ships used to transport cargo from one side of the Atlantic to the other.

"Year after year in quiet calm office-rooms," describes James Pope-Hennessey, "in a myriad European seaports, the thoughtful plans were laid out. The aim of these plans was to make money."[22] Their success relied on slavers, who wedged hundreds of enslaved Africans into the holds of slave ships, sailed to the Americas, and sold the captives in New World slave markets.

A typical route began in a European or an American port, such as Liverpool in England, Lisbon in Portugal, or Bristol in Rhode Island. There, crew members loaded the ships with goods to trade in exchange for slaves. The vessels, often called slavers or Guineamen, then sailed to Africa. Pope-Hennessey describes two-masted brigs, sails blown full by the wind, heading "southward, down the steamy western coast of Africa, rounding Cape Verde, turning due east at Cape Palmas into the Gulf of Guinea. Here at selected points with names far more romantic than the sordid realities of the mud towns that bear them, a slave ship cast anchor."[23]

Once in Africa, slavers bought Africans with the goods they brought. When Olaudah Equiano was sold to a European slaver, he might have been part of a group of a hundred captives, purchased for such items as cowrie shells, guns, cloth, hats, rum, glass beads, or gold.

Although those items were valuable in Africa, their abundance did not necessarily ensure speedy trade. On one voyage a captain might quickly find traders willing to swap goods for slaves. On another, however, he might have to wait weeks or months before filling his ship. According to Pope-Hennessey,

Sometimes the ships filled quickly, and the wooden shelves, which the carpenters erected in the holds now empty of European merchandise, would be crammed with [chained African captives] lying . . .

"like books upon a shelf." . . . At other times the slave ship would lie off the glittering coast of Benin or Biafra for months . . . "waiting to be slaved."[24]

Records show that slave ships the size of large modern-day sailboats might have carried as many as six hundred captives in one voyage. Finally, jam-packed with valuable people, as one callous slaver trader called them, slave ships set sail across the Atlantic Ocean bound for the West Indies, Brazil, or the southern ports of North America.

During the crossing diseases such as smallpox and a violent form of dysentery, called the bloody flux, often decimated the captives. "In the worst ships," says Pope-Hennessey, "in which the slave-holds were not properly aired, nor the floors and shelves washed down with pailfuls of vinegar; in

The Royal African Company and Slaves in the New World

For more than one hundred years, the Royal African Company financed slave ships that brought Africans to the New World. Founded by a royal charter in 1672, the Royal African Company was governed by its largest shareholder, James, duke of York, brother to the king of England. According to Hugh Thomas in *The Slave Trade*, on the list of people who gave money to start the company, "there were four members of the royal family, two dukes, a marquis, five earls, four barons, and seven knights."

The participation of those investors directly connected the English government to the slave trade and this tie had a major impact on the development of the British colonies in the New World. Because the profits of the Royal African Company directly affected the ruling class, promoting the use of slaves in North America and the New World greatly benefited the English government.

In *Black Cargoes*, Daniel P. Mannix and Malcolm Cowley explain, "Since the Royal African Company was launched under protection of the Crown and contributed to the fortunes of the royal family, the government itself encouraged the colonies to buy slaves. . . . It was not until after the Royal African Company was chartered in 1672 that the North American slave trade began to flourish." Mannix and Cowley estimate that, in 1650, there were only three hundred slaves in Virginia. By 1700, however, England's southern colonies were importing slaves at at rate of a thousand a year, many directly from Africa.

Europeans view slaves for sale in Brazil about 1850. Slaves in Brazil were often used to work in gold and silver mines.

which the slaves were not properly fed and exercised; in which the crew were bestial and drunken,"[25] Africans died at an alarming rate.

After as little as three weeks or as long as three months, the ships reached their ports. Plantation owners in the Caribbean and throughout the southern United States then bought the Africans. In Brazil, wealthy Europeans who owned gold and silver mines purchased slaves to mine these precious ores. In other parts of South America, slaves worked on coffee and cacao plantations.

Once slave ships were emptied of their human cargo, they were reloaded with commodities such as sugar, cocoa, rice, gold, silver, copper, and rum and returned to their ports of origin. Crew members and dockworkers unloaded the items into warehouses, where they would be stored and sold at a healthy profit. And, remarks Pope-Hennessey, "the third side of the triangle was complete."[26]

Investors

Clearly, the European demand for goods produced in the New World helped fuel the slave trade. However, it was the financial backing of financiers and investors that made the Atlantic slave trade possible.

An eighteenth-century slaving expedition required a substantial sum of money, roughly the equivalent of three hundred thousand dollars in today's market. To raise that money, businessmen pooled their funds and formed partnerships. Generally six or seven partners made up an investment group. Some business partners were extremely wealthy landowning members of society; others were part of government-sponsored slave trading companies such as the Dutch West Indies Company or England's Royal African Company.

Once investors agreed to finance a trip, the group needed to obtain a ship. If an investor were a shipbuilder or owned a ship, the matter was settled. Otherwise, a merchant ship was procured. In general, though, shipwrights merely converted cargo ships into slavers.

Taking advantage of the wealth that the New World offered motivated Europeans to uproot themselves and move to the Americas. Settlers soon realized that they needed cheap labor to grow the crops and mine the precious ores that sold for great sums of money in Europe. African slaves provided that labor force. Colonizing the Americas to increase Europe's riches fueled the growth of the African slave trade.

The Journey to Africa

During the eighteenth century, trading slaves was a lucrative business. Generally, it promised substantial returns on money invested and therefore interested a wide variety of people wanting to make a profit. Some were members of the church or held important government positions. Others were involved in charitable activities, such as giving great sums of money to help the poor. Hat makers, pawnbrokers, even widows who wanted to increase a small inheritance, all invested in slave trading. Businessmen invested in slaves the way that people today buy and sell stocks in the stock market. "We sold Captain Wanton's cargo . . . at £36 and 35 sterling round [roughly $173 and $158]," reported one slave trader, "but they were prime, and such slaves will always meet a good and ready market. Slaves have been high at Carolina, but by the last accounts they were fallen."[27]

The Captain

Investors wanted the assurance that their investment would be profitable. As a result, they sought captains who were familiar with slave ship life and would protect and manage their investments well. At sea, the captain's responsibilities were many. Navigating the ship across the Atlantic was just one. He had to be strong enough to withstand the storms at sea and to navigate when equipment broke during the crossing. He had to have the presence of mind to handle difficult crew members and be able to negotiate prices for slaves with African kings and slave merchants.

On board, the captain's authority stood unchallenged. Wrote John Newton, an eighteenth-century slave ship captain, in a letter to his wife, "I am as absolute in my small dominions as any potentate [great power] in Europe. If I say to one, come, he comes; if to another, go, he flies. . . . Not a man in the ship will eat his dinner till I please to give him leave."[28]

However, the position of slave ship captain was not considered a career because slaving was a grueling experience. As Captain Newton remarked, "In general, I know of no method of getting money, not even that of robbing for it upon the highway, which has so direct a tendency . . . to rob the heart of every gentle and human disposition, and to harden it, like steel."[29]

Professional maritime officers rarely journeyed to Africa more than once. Only the strongest signed on again to face once more the exhausting schedule, the poor living conditions, turbulent crews and slaves, as well as the devastating tropical diseases that often left permanent physical damage, such as blindness or deafness. Captain Thomas Phillips commented about his life as captain aboard the slaver the *Hannibal:* "No gold-finders can endure so much noisome slavery as they do who carry negroes. . . . We pine and fret ourself to death, and take so much pains to so little purpose."[30]

Being captain of a slave ship was such a harsh experience that few captains made more than one trip.

Hiring the Crew

Once hired himself, the captain set about hiring a crew. "Nothing is more difficult than to procure a sufficient number of hands for a Guinea voyage,"[31] wrote James F. Stanfield, a veteran seamen who made several trips to Africa during the early 1700s. To outfit a slave ship, the captain often required as much as double the number of crew members normally needed to sail a ship trading in other goods; however, maintaining a large crew increased security on the African coast and during the Middle Passage. Some crews numbered as few as fifteen; others could contain as many as forty-five men.

Seamen regularly walked the waterfront in search of work. Sometimes a seamen would ask crew members on board if the captain needed sailors. For example, William Gittus, a young man hoping for a position on a slave ship, went down to Shadwell Dock on the River Thames in 1717, eyed a likely vessel, went aboard, and asked the mate "whither she [the ship] was bound and whether she wanted any hands and what Wages her master gave."[32]

News of an upcoming expedition also spread by word of mouth. Although the ship's captain was hired for his expertise, the crew was generally a lower caliber of sailor. Frequently captains sat themselves at tables in harbor taverns or on decks of the ships and signed up their crews. Captain John Newton remarked: "We are for the most part supplied with the refuse and dregs of the nation. The prisons and glass houses [pubs] furnish us with large quotas of boys impatient of their parents or masters, or already ruined by some untimely vice and for the most part devoid of all good principles."[33]

The portrait of the degenerate crew member aboard a slave ship does appear frequently in the records of slavers and mariners. However, some historians believe that the men and boys who staffed these vessels were, "in almost equal proportions, sailors down on their luck and young landsmen with romantic notions about the slave trade."[34]

To become crew members, sailors signed their names—or, if they were illiterate, made their mark—on a contract detailing their position, rate of pay, and sometimes the destination and purpose of the voyage. Generally, the crew was divided into officers, seamen, and specialists.

With a Nation Behind the Trip

Preparing the slave ship for a voyage involved many areas of a nation's economy. It was not just the slave trader, himself, or the captain of the ship who played a part. Several people contributed, and a great many never sailed a boat or lived close to the ocean.

Farmers, who lived miles inland, grew wheat for the ship's bread and flour supply. They also raised the livestock that fed the crew and captives during the voyage. Owners of ironworks, whose foundries were far away from any slave ship port, supplied iron for the spikes that held the ship together, the chains that bound the captives and the hoops for the storage barrels. From the judge or government official who invested in a slave voyage to the cloth merchant who wove material to be traded for slaves, national involvement in the slave trade was far-reaching.

The extent of these links is especially well illustrated by the numbers of businessmen who protested the legal end of the slave trade. Bakers, who made tons of biscuits for slave ships, asserted that ending the slave trade would bankrupt them. Ironworkers, barrel makers, carpenters, and farmers all claimed that ending the slave trade would hurt them, too.

In *Documents Illustrative of the Slave Trade*, Elizabeth Donnan includes several pieces of evidence to support this idea. For example, a petition signed by the various manufacturers of goods for trade with Africa, presented before the House of Commons in England on May 20, 1789, maintained that, "should the said Trade be abolished, the Petitioners will be injured in their Fortunes and Property, to a very alarming Extent, and many Thousands, who depend on them for Employment and Subsistence, be brought into Poverty and Distress." Shipbuilders; shipowners; sail makers; merchants; dealers in iron, copper, brass, and lead; bakers; rope makers; gun makers; coopers; and block makers were among the other industries that presented petitions on that date to demand that slave trading continue. Even the mayor of Liverpool, a large English slave trading port, presented a petition in favor of slave trading.

This deep involvement in the slave trade might easily apply to other cities throughout Europe and the Americas. The success of a slaving voyage meant profit or loss for people who had never bought a slave, sailed a ship, or even seen the ocean. Yet the outcome of the trip often had a powerful effect on both their livelihoods as well as the economic well-being of their nations.

Officers

Although no one aboard a slave ship held the degree of authority that matched the captain's, the officers were placed directly below the captain within the hierarchy of the ship's chain of command. Not all officers held the same degree of power or received the same rate of pay, though. Senior officers, a rank that included the sailing master and the first mate, had more authority and made more money than petty officers such as the second mate and the boatswain.

While the captain studied the ship's course in his cabin, the rest of the crew ran the ship under the watchful eye of the first mate. Historian Marcus Rediker explains:

The [first] mate whose powers were vastly inferior to those of the [captain], was second in the chain of command. He commanded a watch and oversaw the daily functioning of the ship. He was charged with [managing] the vessel, setting the men to work, governing the crew, securing the cargo, and directing the ship's course. The mate needed a sure knowledge of navigation, since he was to take charge of the vessel in the event of the [captain's] death, no uncommon occurrence at any time during the age of sail.[35]

Slave ships that carried a large crew might also include a second mate. In general,

Seamen James F. Stanfield on Crimping

James F. Stanfield was a seaman who spent many years aboard slave vessels. At the request of the English antislave trade advocate Thomas Clarkson, Stanfield wrote a series of letters describing a sailor's life in the slave trade. The following excerpt is from *Black Voyage,* edited by Thomas Howard. In it, Stanfield depicts how sailors were often tricked into serving aboard a slave ship.

According to Stanfield, one common scheme involved recruiters, otherwise known as crimps, who lured unsuspecting people into debt. Taverns were set up for the purpose of providing crimps with a place to supply boys and young men with food and liquor, pretending to befriend them, get them drunk, and loan them money. More often than not, though, these people were unable to pay back the money, and the crimps had them thrown in jail. The only way immediately available

to gain their freedom was to serve on a slave ship.

"These [taverns] are kept in continual operation. But, at the immediate time of an outfit, every exertion and contrivance is used. Merchants, clerks, captains and others prowl about without intermission. They lay hold of every sailor they meet, and without ceremony, hurry him into some scene of intoxication. I have been dragged into houses three times, in the course of one street myself. Nay, I have known many seamen who fancied themselves cunning enough to evade these practices, go with the crimps to some of their houses, boasting that they would cheat the merchant out of a night's merriment, and firmly resolved to oppose every article that could be offered, yet have they, in their state of drunkenness signed articles with the very men whose purposes they were aware of, and have been plunged into a situation, of which they had known the horrors."

The first mate was second in command and oversaw the daily operations of the ship, supervised the crew, and directed the ship's course.

the crew had little respect for the second mate as an officer. He ate and slept on the quarterdeck cabin, along with the other officers, but he scraped his meals together from the officer leftovers. Sometimes called the sailor's waiter, the second mate had to furnish men with the materials and tools they needed to do their jobs. Richard H. Dana Jr., author of the autobiographical classic *Two Years Before the Mast,* referred to the position as "a dog's berth . . . neither officer or man."[36]

The boatswain, another petty officer, also worked alongside the crew. According to historian Rediker, the boatswain "summoned the crew to [work], sometimes by piping the call . . . that brought the . . . groans and curses from the off-duty crew. His specific responsibilities centered on the upkeep of the rigging. He had to be sure that all lines and cables were sound and that sails and anchors were in good condition."[37]

Specialists

In addition to officers, the slave ship traveled with specialists. These crew members were experts in a particular skill that was vital in the efficient running of a slave ship.

Ship carpenters were particularly valued specialists. "The carpenter, an important specialist in a wooden world, was responsible for the soundness of the ship," remarks Rediker.

He repaired masts, yards, boats, machinery; he checked the hull regularly, placing oakum between the seams of planks, and used wooden plugs on leaks to keep the vessel tight. His search for a leak often required that he wade through stagnant bilge water with vapors strong enough "to poison the Devil." His was highly skilled work which he had learned through apprenticeship. Often he had a mate whom he in turn trained.[38]

Another important specialist on board a slave ship was the doctor, sometimes called the surgeon. Keeping both crew and slaves alive and healthy benefited business, and, as a result, the doctor was involved in major decisions about the voyage. The medicines in his chest included gum, camphor, pulverized rhubarb, cinnamon, water, mustard, and bitters, a bitter liquid made with herbs or roots that was used as a tonic. Most of these substances had little or no power to cure some of the deadly diseases that afflicted those on board. However, the doctor did have some effective medicines. For instance, Peruvian bark, a substance later used to treat malaria, was a popular medicine for fever-ridden patients.

The gunner, along with his assistant, usually a boy called a powder monkey, manned the artillery to defend the ship against pirates and enemy warships. During a battle at sea, the gunner supervised the firing of cannons, diverting disastrous accidents such as a cannon bursting, overheating, or recoiling out of control.

The powder monkey (such as this one from a nineteenth-century warship) assisted the gunner in operating the cannons to defend the ship.

Able-bodied seamen performed the more challenging tasks while ordinary seamen and boys handled the menial chores.

Sometimes called the captain's servant, the steward managed the food supply during the voyage. He reported directly to the captain, overstepping the first mate. Dana points out that breaking the chain of command often caused conflict between the steward and the first mate. Furthermore, reports Dana, "the crew [did] not consider him as one of their number, so he [was] left to the mercy of the captain."[39]

During the eighteenth century, many people, including some captains, were illiterate. To make sure that investors were aware of all business transactions, slave ships also employed an agent or accountant, who recorded the goods traded for slaves, their cost, and the number of slaves obtained through each business deal.

Seamen

The success of the voyage relied on the abilities of the lowliest members of its workforce—the seamen. These sailors were divided into two groups: able-bodied seamen, who were experienced, and ordinary seamen, who, regardless of age, were assigned the most menial tasks because they had no training or experience. Historian W. Jeffrey Bolster explains that it was the sailors who categorized themselves: "Individual sailors rated themselves as able seaman, ordinary seaman, or 'boys' when they signed the ship's articles."[40]

Likewise, the seamen themselves usually decided who performed which task. From helm rotation to lookouts, the officers rarely intervened. To do so might invite the men's disrespect because a seaman considered it an insult to assign him a job he thought was beneath his ability. Therefore, the able-bodied seamen, says Bolster, were given "the most challenging jobs . . . those that demand the neatest work. An able seaman could be ordered by the mate to sweep the decks or to pick oakum, but if there were boys around and true seamen's work was going on elsewhere, such a task would be considered punishment."[41]

The Fear of Desertion

Once signed on, a sailor might live on the ship until it set sail. Historians Daniel P. Mannix and Malcolm Cowley explain that "it was the custom for a [slave ship] to lie in the out harbor of a . . . port, sometimes for weeks, until it had assembled a crew."[42] During that time, sailors helped with the numerous duties in preparing the ship for departure.

The poor treatment of sailors aboard slave ships was notorious, but while the ship was in the harbor, the captain and officers made sure to give seamen ample food, drink, and leisure time. It was all too easy for sailors

Making Sea Voyages More Accurate

Today, charting a course across the ocean is far less challenging than it was in the eighteenth century when slave traders navigated the seas. Technology such as radios and radar helps modern sailors determine their location, but three hundred years ago, sailors had to rely on less accurate instruments to guide them.

Two inventions during the eighteenth century, however, vastly improved sea travel. In the mid-1700s, English clockmaker John Harrison invented the chronometer, which carried true time on voyages around the world. Knowing the true time aboard ship and at the home port helped determine a ship's location and prevented sailors from getting lost at sea.

Fifty years later American seaman, Nathaniel Bowditch developed an accurate way to determine a ship's position on the ocean. For centuries, sailors had relied on a nautical instrument called a sextant for that purpose. The sextant, however, based its information on the position of the moon and other planets and as a result, was not very accurate. Searching for more dependable methods, Bowditch began to update the sailing industry's nautical guides. In the process, he uncovered so many mistakes in the original book that, in 1802, he published his own manual, *The New Practical Navigator*. The updated guide made sailing across the sea less hazardous because it made it easier for sailors to stay on course. A revised version of Bowditch's guide is still being used today.

Hogsheads, large barrels used to store food and trade goods, sit alongside a ship. The crew sometimes lived aboard the ship while preparing it for the journey.

to jump ship and swim ashore if conditions became as intolerable as they often were once at sea. As crew member James F. Stanfield describes it,

> Til the vessel gets clear of the channel—till there is no probability that contrary winds or inclemency of weather will drive her back into an English port, the usage of the seamen is moderate, and their allowance of provisions sufficient; in short, the conduct of the captain and officers appears like that which is the continual practice in every other employ. But as soon as they are fairly out at sea . . . their rations of provisions is shorted to the very verge of famine.[43]

Slave Ship Design

A typical slave ship was made of wooden planks fastened together by long iron spikes. Compared with modern ships, slavers were surprisingly small. Usually they were seventy-five feet long with a cargo capacity of under three hundred tons, the size of a modern fishing schooner, and had three masts. Each mast held two square-shaped canvas sails. The sails were tied to the masts by ropes, or rigs, as they were called. The middle and tallest mast was called the mainmast; the mast in the front, or bow, of the boat was called the foremast. The back, or stern, of the boat had a mast called the mizzenmast, from which flew a small triangular sail.

There were two decks, one above and one below, which were used to store slaves and other goods. The one above, known as the main deck, was also called the weather deck because it was exposed to wind and weather. On the bow of the ship there was a

Captain John Newton and Captain Hugh Crow

Different people viewed the slave trade in different ways. Some who made their living as slave traders had mixed feelings about what they were doing. The English captain John Newton gave up slaving in 1754, after nearly ten years at sea, and devoted the rest of his life to ending the slave trade. He became an Anglican clergyman, and he used his pulpit to preach against slavery. He also wrote a condemning memoir of the slave trade, gave forceful testimony before the House of Commons to support the abolition of slavery, and composed several popular hymns, including "Amazing Grace."

In one 1797 sermon, excerpted in Thomas Howard's *Black Voyage*, Newton says, "If the trade is at present carried on to the same extent and nearly in the same manner, while we are delaying to put a stop to our part in it, the blood of many thousands of our helpless, much injured fellow creatures is crying against us."

Not everyone agreed with Newton, however. As historian Hugh Thomas observes in *The Slave Trade*, slave ship captain Hugh Crow believed "the abstractions of slaves to our colonies [was] a necessary evil," and "seem[ed] sincerely convinced that the African slaves in the West Indies were happier than when they lived as slaves in their own country, 'subject to the caprices [impulsive actions] of their native princes.'"

A native of the Isle of Man, located in the Irish Sea off the coast of Great Britain, Crow earned an excellent reputation in the industry because of his sailing and navigating skill and his ability to keep losses of sailors and slaves down. He was also known as a scrappy fighter when challenged. Apparently he had lost an eye in a fight when he was twelve years old, and his name came from the one-eyed crowlike squint he gave people.

As a captain, Crow prided himself on his treatment of his slave cargoes. He was reportedly one of the few who taught slaves to shoot and used them in times of attack to help repel the enemy. Crow said he never regretted the practice; the entrusted slaves were always loyal to him despite the loaded guns in their hands.

In 1807 Hugh Crow sailed the last legal slave trading voyage out of Liverpool, England. Although Parliament had outlawed the trade on May 1, the owner of the ship, the *Kitty Amelia*, had cleared the ship's articles before that time. On July 27 the ship set sail, and by the time it docked in St. Thomas, fifty slaves and thirty seamen had died. "Crow was dejected," reports Thomas Howard in *Black Voyage*. "He had a reputation of running a clean ship and the deaths depressed him. The despondent Crow retired on the savings made during his seafaring days to his native Isle of Man, where he wrote his autobiography."

After the preparations were complete, the time to set sail was determined based on the route, season, weather, and crop harvest.

small enclosed structure called a forecastle, often abbreviated as *foc's'le*. The crew slept in the forecastle and the officers slept in cabins located in the back, or aft.

Finally, most slave ships were armed with between eight to twelve guns and a chest of small arms such as muskets and pistols. Seamen used these arms to defend themselves against pirates who tried or actually managed to climb aboard. Sometimes officers used weapons to subdue a mutinous crew or rebellious group of African captives.

Preparing the Ship

Slave ships were kept docked in the ports of Europe and the Americas, waiting for the next voyage. During the mid- and late-1700s, the height of the slave trade, a walk along the wharves in Providence, Rhode Island, or London revealed just how popular the industry was. As one writer describes it, "the muddy brown waters [of the harbor] would become so choked with slave ships, seamen could cross it by stepping from ship deck to ship deck."[44]

Preparing a ship sometimes took as long as six months. Dockworkers and sailors scraped, sanded, and oiled the planks on the ship's deck and hull. On board, sailors packed planking with a mixture of tar and a type of caulk called oakum to keep the ship watertight. Carpenters rebuilt decks and made storage space for goods to be traded. Sail makers mended torn sails, and riggers replaced old ropes, cables, and pulleys.

Barnacles and shipworms continually ate away at the wood of the vessel. Dockyard workers, including children hoping to earn a few pennies, scraped barnacles from the hull of the ship and scrubbed old ship ropes. Work crews hammered down loose wood with iron spikes and renovated the galley to accommodate the copper stove, a large shallow bowl surrounded by bricks to keep the fire underneath from spreading throughout the ship.

As some crew members repaired the ship, others loaded the goods for the expedition. Heavy wooden carts pulled by oxen drove along the waterfront's cobblestone streets carrying barrels, crates, and casks of goods for the voyage. Provisions were divided into three categories: goods for trading, food and drink for crew and captive consumption, and equipment.

Large barrels used for storage and transport were called hogsheads and could hold roughly 63 to 140 gallons. On the slave ship *Cleopatra,* captain James Bourk sailed with 234 hogsheads of New England rum and one thousand hogsheads of hops, a grain used to make ale, which he hoped to trade for slaves. In addition, the ships were stocked with iron bars, glass beads, pewter ware, linen and calico cloth, indigo cloth dye, paint, and guns. The seamen turned hoisting devices on board the ship, called windlasses, which helped lift the big hogsheads of goods. The windlasses creaked and groaned as sailors swung the heavy containers of provisions aboard and lowered them into the hold—the lowest part of the ship, for storage.

To feed the crew and slaves, the *Cleopatra* carried eleven hogsheads and one small cask of chickpeas, two barrels of wine, sixty-four kegs of water biscuits, six casks of Indian corn, a large cask of a special type of ham known as gammon, two hogsheads of black-eyed peas, six tierce [casks] and two hogsheads of rice, twenty barrels of common flour, ten barrels of superfine flour, and eight casks of bread.

Some ships sailed with live turkeys, chickens, and even cattle on board to be used for food during the journey. In addition to fresh drinking water and wine, the latter of which each man received a quart and a half per day, rum, tobacco, and brandy were staples in the ship's store.

Captain Bourk brought great lengths of rope; a variety of anchors; six barrels each of tar, pitch, and turpentine; two half barrels of gunpowder; and 670 feet of white oak boards and 330 feet of red oak to make shelves, or ledges, for the slaves. His provisions also included heavy chains, iron collars, at least one hundred pairs of iron shackles for wrists and ankles, and sharp tools used to force-feed African captives who refused to eat.

Safely stowed in the captain's quarters were the ship's documents. The packet of documents included a manifest, which listed the cargo and crew members on board; a certificate of clearance papers, which certified that the ship's equipment and cargo had been inspected and gave the captain permission to leave the harbor; a bill of health for crew members; and trading instructions from the investors, to be used upon arrival in Africa.

As the captain and officers stood on the weather deck barking orders, the crew scurried about following their commands. Some sailors turned the windlass to pull up, or weigh, anchor. Others worked the rigging. Block and tackle (a pulley of ropes and cables for hoisting heavy objects) squeaked as the seamen angled the sails to catch the wind.

When to Set Sail

Once loaded with provisions, fully repaired, and made watertight, with captain and crew hired, the slave ship was read to set sail.

Planning the best time to embark on the journey across the Atlantic depended on a number of factors, including weather and crop harvest. It also depended on the point of departure. Sailing from Charleston, South Carolina, to Africa required one schedule, sailing from London another.

According to James Barbot, an English slave ship captain, the last two weeks in September were ideal to begin the voyage from London to Guinea, a slave trading country on Africa's west coast. Barbot advised,

> I Am of opinion that the properest season to render the Guinea voyages most prosperous and safe, is to depart from Europe about the latter end of September, to enjoy . . . the good season on that coast; and to have a sufficient time to carry on the trade there, so as to reach the Leeward islands of America by the latter end of April following, which is the time when they make the sugar there; so ships may have their full lading [load], and sail thence for Europe again before the season of hurricanes there; and arrive here, before the boisterous weather, which usually reigns on our coasts about the beginning of October.[45]

Making the first leg of the Triangle of Trade demanded a great deal from captain and crew. The unpredictability of the weather and the often violent temper of the captain made seamen feel constantly on edge. Courageous and dependable yet rowdy and difficult to discipline, the sailors themselves were a varied group. Yet, their seafaring skills played a vital role in the slave trade, specifically, and transatlantic trade as a whole.

Capturing the Slaves

After about a month or two of sailing, the African shore appeared. As the ship headed down the windward coast toward the Gulf of Guinea, it passed by several slave trading ports. These were the towns Anamabu, Accra, and Ouidah, through which captives such as Ottobah Cugoano, a young Fantee boy who was kidnapped and sold into slavery, passed as they became the ship's human cargo.

It was on their way to the slave forts, sometimes called slave castles—where slaves were imprisoned until loaded onto slavers—that captives like Cugoano first witnessed the brutality that would soon become a daily occurrence for them aboard a slave ship. In his memoirs, published in 1789, many years after he was captured, Cugoano recalled,

My guide and kidnapper told me that he had to go to the castle with some company that were going there . . . to get some goods. . . . The horrors I soon saw and felt, cannot be well described; I saw many of my miserable countrymen chained two and two, some handcuffed, and some with their hands tied behind. When we arrived at the castle, I saw [my kidnapper] take a gun, a piece of cloth, and some lead [to trade] for me, and then he told me that he must now leave me there, and went off. This made me cry bitterly.[46]

Captured Africans are marched to a slave fort, where slaves were held until their transfer to the ships.

European slave merchants buy an African chief's prisoners of war. The ritual of breaking trade might include buying a certain number of the local king or chief's own slaves.

The last glimpses these slaves had of Africa were the prisons and slave ports. Cugoano described the wrenching experience:

I was soon conducted to a prison, for three days, where I heard the groans and cries of many, and saw some of my fellow-captives. But when a vessel arrived to conduct us away to the ship, there was nothing to be heard but the rattling of chains, smacking of whips, and the groans and cries of our fellow-men. Some [refused to get up and board the ship, even] when they were lashed and beat in the most horrible manner.[47]

Cugoano was taken aboard a slaver that remained on the African coast for several days. The ship stopped at Cape Coast Castle to transfer its human cargo to another ship and finally set sail across the Atlantic. "And when we found ourselves at last taken away," lamented Cugoano, "death was more preferable than life."[48]

Breaking Trade

Before they bought Africans to stock their ships, European traders participated in a ritual called breaking trade. The procedures for breaking trade varied, depending upon the

Venture Smith

In 1798 Venture Smith published his memoir *A Narrative of the Life and Adventures of Venture, a Native of Africa by Resident about Sixty Years in the United States of America,* a portion of which has been excerpted in *Afro-American History: Primary Sources,* edited by Thomas R. Frazier. Smith had purchased freedom for himself as well as his wife and children and lived in East Haddam, Connecticut. Even though he was enslaved and taken from Africa when he was six years old, Smith's memoir gives an accurate and vital description of his capture and reveals how the trade relied on war among tribes to supply slaves.

"The army of the enemy was large, I should suppose consisting of about six thousand men. Their leader was called Baukurre. . . . The enemy had remarkable success in destroying the country wherever they went. For as far as they had penetrated, they laid the habitations waste and captured the people. The distance they had now brought me was about four hundred miles. On the march [to the sea] the prisoners were treated with clemency, on account of their being submissive and humble. Having come to the next tribe, the enemy laid siege and immediately took men, women, [and] children. . . . They then went on to the next district which was contiguous to [touching] the sea, called in Africa, Anamaboo. The inhabitants . . . attacked and took [the] enemy [army] and [their] prisoners. . . . [Thus] I was then taken a second time. All of us were then put into the castle, and kept for market. On a certain time, I and other prisoners were put on board a canoe, under our master, and rowed away to a vessel belonging to Rhode Island, commanded by Captain Collingwood, and the mate Thomas Mumford. While we were going to the vessel, our master told us all to appear to the best possible advantage for sale. I was bought on board by one Robertson Mumford, steward of said vessel, for four gallons of rum, and a piece of calico, and called 'Venture,' on account of his having purchased me with his own private venture."

customs, tastes, and needs of each region along the slave coast. However, there was one constant: Regardless of where traders landed, all ships needed a license to buy slaves. To obtain a license, the slave ship captain paid a fee to a local king or chief. The fee might include purchasing a specified number of the chief's own slaves or giving the local chief gifts.

The slave ship cast anchor about a mile outside the town, and the captain rowed ashore with two or three crew members. Slave ship surgeon Alexander Falconbridge described how

sometimes fifteen [ships], English and French . . . meet here [on the coast of Nigeria near Bonny] together. Soon they cast anchor, the captains go on shore to make known their arrival. . . . They likewise invite the kings of Bonny to come on board, to whom . . . they usually make presents which generally consist of pieces of cloth, cotton, chintz, silk, handkerchiefs and . . . sometimes brandy, wine or beer.[49]

Slave traders tried to comply with the demands of their suppliers to avoid any complications that might delay trading. By the mid-eighteenth century, permission to trade might cost as much as £400, slightly under two thousand dollars in today's currency.

Once the license was obtained, gun shots might be fired to announce the beginning of trading. Reports Falconbridge, "After the kings have been on board and have received the usual presents, permission is granted by them for trafficking with any of the black traders. When the royal guests return from the ships they are saluted by the guns."[50]

Building the "House" on Deck

While the captain negotiated with traders on shore, the crew started preparing the ship for slave trading by building a "house" on board. Slavers used the house as a pen for the physical examination and branding of the newly purchased captives.

First, they unbent the sails, which meant they untied them. Then, the seamen struck the yards and topmasts—in other words, the crew hauled them down. After that, the seaman lashed yards and other wooden poles from mast to mast to form a ridgepole, the horizontal beam running along the top point of the roof. Inside the house, the crew used a pine board to build a wall with a door.

A wall segregated the male and female captives, and sometimes slaves were kept in the house as a way to prevent them from jumping overboard. For added security, small openings in the thatched walls allowed the crew to keep a small cannon or gun pointed at the slaves at all times. A trap door in the roof of the house permitted the crew to lower food down to the captives.

An agent (in white hat) looks over his newly acquired slaves as their stocks are removed. Agents were employed by captains to buy slaves directly from African traders.

However, the house offered little protection from the brutal weather. The mat roofing leaked during rainstorms, and rather than providing shelter from the glaring sun, the house was extremely hot and the close air unhealthy. In addition, the smoke from the green mango-wood fires, which were necessary to heat the branding irons, stung the sailors' eyes and was even known to cause blindness.

Some seamen considered making the house the most terrible experience of the journey. To cut down the mangrove branches, reeds, and bamboo shoots for the walls and roof, sailors waded waist deep in swamp mud. The men, who were often ill and feverish, did this work in the intense tropical heat, as mosquitoes swarmed about and poisonous snakes slithered beside them.

Agents and Middlemen

Although some captains sailed up and down the coast, traveling from trading post to trading post and buying slaves along the way, many others employed men called agents to obtain slaves for them. Agents were Europeans who lived in Africa and worked for slave trading companies. Their job was to buy slaves directly from African slave traders and have cargoes ready for loading. Another name for agent was factor, and the holding pens where they kept their slaves were called factories.

Fevers on the African Coast

In his memoir, published in London in 1807, James F. Stanfield describes his experiences as a crew member of a slave ship anchored along the Guinea coast. The following passage, excerpted from *Black Voyage*, edited by Thomas Howard, recounts the agonizing deaths that European slavers suffered when tropical fevers swept through their ships.

"At the commencement of our trade, I went up to the [holding pens where slaves were kept], where I continued about eight months. In the course of this time most of the crew fell [to] the sacrifices of this horrid traffick and its inseparable cruelties. One evening only was I on board during this period. . . . The chief mate lay dying, calling out for that comfort and assistance he had so often denied to others. He was glad to lay hold of me to bring him a little refreshment—no one else would take the smallest notices of his cries. The doctor was in the same condition, and making the same complaint. The second mate was lying on his back on the medicine-chest, his head hanging down over one end of it, his hair sweeping the deck and clotted with the filth that was collected there, and in this unnoticed situation he died soon after I came on board. . . . On the [deck at the stern] the appearance was still more shocking—the remainder of the ship's crew stretched in the last stage of their sickness, without comfort, without refreshment, without attendance. There they lay, straining their weak voices with the most lamentable cries for a little water, and not a soul to afford them the smallest relief. And while all this horror and disease were preying on the lives of the poor seamen, the business of purchasing . . . was transacting with as little interruption, and as much unconcern as if no such people had ever been on board."

European traders acquired slaves through raids (pictured) or by purchasing prisoners of war.

Nicholas Owen, one of the few European factors to leave a diary, described his life trading slaves on the African coast. He represented a typical white trader who came to the Guinea coast to recover a family fortune lost through gambling, bad investments, and drink. He was not successful, and the riches he hoped to gain trading slaves never materialized. The hot, fever-ridden climate of Africa weakened his health, and he died at thirty-three years of age in 1759 from a tropical disease. However, the journal he left behind is valuable because it describes the life of an African factor, including the failure many traders experienced trying to trade slaves.

As historian Thomas Howard points out, "Nowhere in his journal does [Owen] express repugnance of the trade or show any concern for the inhumanity shown the slaves."[51] Rather, Howard explains that Owen's journal entries often focus on his physical hardships and inability to make money by trading slaves. In one entry, Owen writes

> In this place I find several ugly things . . . such as long worms and frogs; the latter make such horrid noises in the night that it breaks my sleep. Last night I found one of these worms eight or nine inches long under my bed, which was the occasion of my not sleeping until 11 or 12 a clock. . . . I live here, but not with so much strength as I was want in Europe or any cold climate; my bones seem weaker and in hot weather I am [feverish]. What most troubles me is the musquetos [mosquitoes] at

night, and in the day large flies [take] their places. . . . The bite of one of these flies is so penetrating that your shirt will hardly keep it out.[52]

Typical of European agents, Owen set up his business on Sherbro Island at the mouth of the Sherbro River, a major trading site in Sierra Leone, Africa. Europeans often purchased slaves by setting up stalls and slave depots along such rivers, and when slave traffic was slow on the coast, the agent employed Africans to travel inland to trade for slaves. Slaver John Barbot described the practice: "If there happens to be no stock of slaves . . . the factor must trust the blacks with his goods, to the value of one hundred and fifty, or two hundred pounds [English currency]; which goods they carry up into the inland country, to buy slaves at all markets, for about six hundred miles up the country, where they are kept like cattle in Europe."[53]

In addition, the mulatto offspring of European traders and African women played an active role in procuring slaves. They worked as middlemen. Historian Edward Reynolds explains that, in certain areas such as the Gold Coast, mulatto children grew up in slave ports directly connected to slave fortresses. Under the influence of a slave trading environment, they often served as interpreters for African chieftains selling slaves or worked for European agents. Sometimes they, too, became slave traders and sold directly to European slavers.

Capturing Africans: Prisoners of War

There were two ways African chieftains and slave traders obtained the captives they sold

to European slavers. The first and most common method according to some historians, was by taking prisoners of war. Captain John Barbot, who bought slaves in Senegambia at the beginning of the 1800s, wrote in his memoirs that "those sold . . . are for the most part prisoners of war, taken either in flight, or pursuit, or in the incursions they make into their enemies' territories."[54]

The African King as Trader

In 1820, thirteen years after England's abolition of the slave trade, Osei Bonsu, king of Africa's Ashanti empire, which covered the Gold Coast and spread deep into Africa, explained his method of capturing Africans to sell to European traders. In an interview with British representative Joseph Dupuis, excerpted from David Northrup's *The Atlantic Slave Trade*, Bonsue remarks on the relationship between war and slaves.

"I cannot make war to catch slaves in the bush, like a thief. My ancestors never did so. But if I fight a king and kill him when he is insolent, then certainly I must have his gold, and his slaves, and the people are mine too. . . . I hear the old men say, that before I conquered Fantee and killed the Braffoes and the kings . . . white men came in great ships, and fought and killed many people; and then they took the gold and slaves to the white country. . . . When I fought Gaman, I did not make war for slaves, but because Dinkera (the king) sent me an arrogant message and killed my people, and refused to pay me gold as his father did."

Some slave traders viewed the slave trade as provoking war among African tribes. Spurred by greed and the promise of increasing its wealth and supply of firearms, one tribe might make war on another. Some experts and eyewitnesses believe that the sole reason for waging war was to sell the defeated tribe to European slave traders. Captain John Newton, for example, a repentant slave ship captain, directly blamed the slave trade for increased tribal warfare during the eighteenth century. As he noted, "I verily believe, that the far greater part of the wars, in Africa, would cease, if the Europeans would cease to tempt them, by offering goods for slaves."[55]

Newton was not alone in connecting warfare among African tribes with the supplying of slaves to European slave traders. In 1724 a slave ship surgeon aboard a slaver who found himself waiting in Africa for weeks, made the following journal entry on December 29: "No trade today, though many traders came on board; They informed us, that the people are gone to war within land, and will bring prisoners enough in two or three days; in hope of which we stay." The following day his entry reads, "No trade yet, but our traders came on board today and informed us the people had burnt four towns of their enemies, so that tomorrow we expect slaves."[56]

Capturing Africans: Kidnapping

Another way slaves were obtained was through kidnapping, also called *panyarring*. Anyone found alone in an isolated place risked the possibility of being kidnapped. Children were especially in danger of being abducted. Olaudah Equiano and Ottobah Cugoano were two kidnapped Africans who left vivid descriptions of their abductions. Equiano and his sister were seized from their home, and the kidnappers carried them to a nearby wood before they were able to cry for help. Once hidden in the wood, "they tied our hands, and continued to carry us as far as they could, til night came on."[57]

Cugoano, too, said he was

> snatched . . . with about eighteen or twenty more boys and girls, as we were playing in the field. . . . Several great ruffians came upon us suddenly, and said we had committed a fault against their lord, and we must go and answer for it ourselves before him. Some of us attempted, in vain, to run away, but pistols and cutlasses were soon introduced, threatening, that if we offered to stir, we should all lie dead on the spot.[58]

Whether kidnapped in a straightforward manner like Equiano or concealed in pretense as in the case of Cugoano, the result was the same. All captives were taken to coastal towns and boarded onto slave ships, where they were sold, enslaved, and transported to the New World.

Buying Slaves and Holding Captives

Regardless of how they were obtained, slaves were brought from inland areas to the coast and were chained together to prevent their escape. Francis Moore, an English agent who worked along the Gambia River, described the method of transport: "Their way of bringing them is tying them by the neck with leather thongs, at about a yard distance from each other, thirty or forty in a string, having generally a bundle of corn or elephants' teeth upon each of their heads."[59]

Upon reaching the coast, captives were herded into fortresslike structures, where they were kept until sold. Once sold, they were branded with the name or mark of their owner and were then returned to the fortress until the European slave trader was ready to sail for the Americas.

Conditions in these forts were horrible. Slaves were given very little to eat. They were crowded into small areas, and often there was no place to go to the bathroom. The smell was terrible, and people who showed any resistance were beaten.

In his memoirs, published in 1705, Captain Willem Bosman describes the way his slave ship crew bought captives:

When the slaves which are brought from the inland countries come to Widah [a slave port on Africa's west coast] they are put in prison together, when we [bargain] concerning buying them, they are all brought out together in a large plain, where by our surgeons, they are thoroughly examined . . . naked both men and women, without the least distinction or modesty. Those which are approved as good are set on one side; in the meanwhile a burning iron, with the arm or name of the company, lies in the fire, with which ours are marked on the breast. . . . They are returned to their prisons, where, from that time forward, they are kept at our charge, and cost us two pence a day each slave, which serves to subsist them like criminals on bread and water.[60]

Transporting Slaves to Slave Ships

The Europeans hired African canoemen from the Gold Coast to ferry slaves and goods to

Slave traders hired African canoemen to transport the slaves to and from the ship.

Africans Retaliate Against European Slavers

Sometimes Africans avenged the capture of friends and family members by kidnapping slave ship crew members and bartering for the release of their loved ones in exchange for their European hostages. As part of his testimony before the House of Commons in 1791, slaver Richard Story described his experience with one such incident of retaliation while traveling in Africa. That testimony was reproduced in *The Atlantic Slave Trade*, edited by David Northrup.

"I once . . . in 1768 . . . was going as a passenger from Lagoo on the Gold Coast to the river Gabon, in one of the trading vessels belonging to the Coast. On the second day . . . two canoes with about twelve or fourteen men came on board with two men bound, which they wanted to sell. When the agreement was made . . . the master of the boat, myself and another White man were all seized—the master's and the other man's throats were both cut immediately. . . . After they had got the major part of the goods out of the boat, they then . . . stripped me naked, put me in a canoe, and took me on shore to their town. . . . The reason they gave me of doing this was, that a ship from Liverpool . . . had taken sometime before a canoe full of their townsmen, and carried them away."

and from the ship, and mariners openly admired the canoemen's skill. As Captain Nathaniel Uring wrote in 1701 during a slaving voyage to Loango,

We saw the Sea break so high, that we began to be afraid to venture and were inclined to return, but the Canow [canoe] People encouraged and assured us there was no Danger. The Canow was large, and had Eight Men to paddle her. . . . When we came near the Breakers they laid still and watched for a Smooth, and then push'd Forward with all their Force, paddling the Canow forward or backward as they saw Occasion, often lying between the Breakers, which was very terrible to see, roaring both before and behind us; when they saw a fair Opportunity they paddled with all their Might toward the Shore and got safe thither.[61]

Yet despite this admiration, many Europeans treated the canoemen with condescen-sion and brutality. Historian W. Jeffrey Bolster reports that, "in 1695, Edward Barter hired a crew of canoemen to ferry corn through the surf. Their canoe overturned, and Barter later beat one of the men 'because he would not help to carry the corn to the croome [a town or village].'"[62] The man's response to Barter's treatment reveals the basic difference between European and African perception. As Barter remembered, "He told me he came to paddle not to carry corn at all."[63] Europeans often described these boatmen as rascally, impudent, or vagabonds. Africans, on the other hand, saw themselves as individuals who made trade agreements on their own terms.

There were, however, some Europeans who recognized the necessity of keeping a good relationship with the canoemen. With his ship anchored a mile and a half off shore, tossed continually by heavy swells, Captain Thomas Phillips was well aware of the risks each time he went ashore. "We venture drowning every time," wrote Phillips, "the canoos [canoes] frequently over-setting, but the canoomen are such excellent divers and swimmers that they preserve the lives of those they have any kindness for. . . . Therefore 'tis very prudent for all commanders to be kind and obliging to them, their lives lying in their hands."[64]

Inspection

Once on board, the slaves were taken into the house the seamen had built on deck. There, a surgeon examined them to make sure they were strong and healthy. Slave captain Theodore Canot later described the detail of the inspection and how discovery of a physical flaw might lower the price of the slave: "A careful manipulation of the chief muscles, joints, armpits and groins was made, to assure soundness. The mouth, too, was inspected, and if a tooth was missing, it was noted as a defect liable to deduction. Eyes, voice, lungs, fingers, and toes were not forgotten."[65]

Slaves were sometimes kept on deck in the open air to preserve their health.

If the surgeon found any defect during his examination, the captain rejected the slave. The master of an unsellable captive frequently beat the slave and sometimes, in certain slave trading posts, such as New Calabar, killed them. Generally, though, these people, known as *Wawa*, meaning "left ones," worked as household slaves for European traders or Africans.

Currency

As the ship filled with slaves, the crew had to make room for its new human cargo. Using simple pulleys and their own strength, seamen hoisted barrels of goods for trading out of the hold and onto the deck. The captain presented the merchandise, and the African slave traders examined the goods as closely as the Europeans examined the slaves.

In addition to trade goods, slave ships carried merchandise that certain Africans considered money. For example, when trading on the eastern Niger delta, captains supplied brass bracelets, called *manillas*, which the people of that area used as currency. In Ouidah, Europeans bought slaves with cowrie shells from the Maldive Islands off the coast of India, and in Senegambia, they used iron bars.

The Length of Time in Africa

Once slavers bought Africans with the currency most valued in that region, the captives were kept either on the ship or in the slave fort until the ship was ready to sail. If the captives remained on the ship while the captain continued to buy Africans to fill his order for slaves, often they were allowed to remain on deck in the open air. The slave deck below

"The Very Best Kind of Slaves"

When slave traders went looking for captives, they set out to find slaves that would sell quickly in the New World. "Let your purchase be of the very best kind of Slaves black and smooth free from blemishes," wrote Charleston-based slave trader Henry Laurens to a colleague about to sail to Africa. His correspondence has been excerpted from Elizabeth Donnan's *Documents Illustrative of the History of the Slave Trade to America.* "Young and well-grown—the more Men the better . . . none sell better than Gambia Slaves."

Males were in greater demand than females. Buyers wanted young slaves—none older than age twenty-five for men and twenty for women. "If you touch any [slaves] below this description," Laurens advised one African trader, "let a very real bargain only tempt you."

According to Laurens, the size of the slave, for example, mattered greatly to the slave buyer of South Carolina. If Africans were too short or too tall, plantation owners would not buy them, and he advised slavers in Africa to let the needs and tastes of the slave buyer in America guide them when filling the slave holds of their ships.

was so foul and suffocating, especially in the heat of the tropical climate, that people forced to lie there often grew very sick or died.

Slave ship captains quickly realized that the longer they took to "slave a ship," the greater the risk of losing slaves and crew members to disease or mutiny. Partly to protect their investment and keep the slaves alive, captains allowed women and children to remain above deck and sometimes men, as long as they were heavily chained.

However, for crew members, allowing slaves on deck brought its own dangers. They feared slaves would rebel, escape, or drown themselves rather than suffer the tortures of European slavery. As a precaution, especially if any escape attempts were made, the ship's officers ordered slaves below deck, even if it meant several deaths.

Like many aspects of slave trading, the amount of time needed to fill a ship varied among regions along the coast. Trading in Sierra Leone might take four to nine months; trading along the Gold Coast could take from six to ten months. In general, however, by 1788 loading a cargo of 450 slaves took from three weeks to three months.

Leaving Africa

As soon as a ship stocked its slave deck with captives, the captain readied it to leave the African Coast. Captain Phillips describes preparing for departure, especially exchanging the necessary formalities between the slave trader (in Phillips's case the king of Ouidah) and the captain:

> Having bought my complement of 700 slaves, 480 men and 220 women, and finish'd all my business at Whidaw [Ouidah] I took my leave of the old king and his cappasheirs [his principal attendants], and parted, with many affectionate expressions on both sides, being forced to promise him that I would return again the next year, with several things he desired me to bring from England.[66]

Emptied of European trading items and packed with Africans, the ship was ready to leave. Crew members dismantled the house on deck, hoisted the masts, tied the rigging, and unfurled the sails. Their course set, the seamen headed back across the Atlantic Ocean for the second leg of the Triangle of Trade, known as the Middle Passage.

4 The Middle Passage

For the captives, setting sail began a journey into the unknown. Many Africans had never seen the ocean before they boarded a slave ship, and the sight frightened them. As Olaudah Equiano explains, "Not being used to the water, I naturally feared the element the first time I saw it."[67]

Equiano's fear of water hardly compared with the journey itself. Confessed one young sailor aboard a French slaving vessel, the cries of the slaves "are so terrible that I do not like to go down and look into the hold. At first I could not close my eyes, the sound froze my

very blood."[68] The suffocating stench of the hold, the brutal beatings of slaves and crew, the perpetual presence of disease and death, all were part of daily life on the slave ship.

Especially unsettling for these Africans was the fact that their destination was unknown. As historian John Henrik Clarke explains, "The manacled and terrified Africans knew very little about the process in which they have been ensnared."[69] Even though Equiano managed to find some captives aboard the slave ship who actually spoke his language and explained to him that they were being taken away to the

A trader walks through the chained slaves below deck. Slave holds were permeated with fear, brutality, disease, and death.

Slaves leap overboard in a desperate attempt to escape the horrors of the slave ship and an uncertain future.

white men's country to work for them, he was still very fearful and suspicious. Equiano, like many Africans, believed the European slavers were cannibals and that he would be taken to a far off country to be eaten.

The terror of the voyage was amplified by the fact that the captives had no idea how long their trip would last. According to Clarke,

> Many of the Africans huddled in the darkness cursed their fate, while others shrieked in horror each time the hatch cover closed above, virtually entombing them. They had no idea what to expect;

what cruel injustices still remained. . . . Having been shipped from their homeland, from their gods, they could only guess what bitter misfortune awaited them.[70]

Torn Away

The agony of being wrenched from the shores of Africa filled the captives with despair. Captain Thomas Phillips witnessed scene after scene of desperate slaves willing to risk death to avoid leaving Africa: "The Negroes are so wilful and loath to leave their own country," he wrote, "that they have often leap'd out of the canoos, boat and ship, into the sea, and kept under water till they were drowned."[71]

From the slaver's point of view, this distress signaled the increased possibility of sickness and death among the slaves. To minimize loss of life and therefore loss of their investment, slave ship captains tried to set sail immediately after slaves boarded the ship. "From the moment that the slaves are embarked, one must put the sails up," advised seventeenth-century French businessman Jacques Savary. "The reason is that these slaves have so great a love for their country that they despair when they see that they are leaving it forever; that makes them die of grief."[72]

Many slave crews took this advice one step further, keeping captives locked below deck in the slave hold until the ship left port. According to one former slave,

> At the time we came into this ship, she was full of black people, who were all confined in a dark and low place in irons. The women were in irons as well as the men. . . . When our prison could hold no more, the ship sailed down the river; and on the night of the second day after she sailed, I heard the roaring of the ocean as it dashed against her sides.[73]

The Slave Deck

Traveling across the ocean below deck was a miserable experience. Slaves were forced to lie down and were chained to one another, the

A Sailor's Schedule: The Watch

Life on a slave ship rotated around the watch. There were six watches in one twenty-four-hour period. All seaman, including officers, stood watch—meaning, they had to complete certain tasks depending on the time of the watch. To make sure that groups alternated tasks and watch hours, the twilight watch—scheduled between 4:00 P.M. and 8:00 P.M.—was split in half: 4:00 P.M. to 6:00 P.M., and 6:00 P.M. to 8:00 P.M. Breaking up the watch was called "dogging the watch."

The second part of the "dog watch" (from 6:00 P.M. to 8:00 P.M.) was the time when the entire crew was on deck. The captain paced the weather side of the quarter deck—the side of the ship facing into the wind—and calculated the ship's location. The first mate

walked on the opposite side of the ship, the lee side, and also read the wind's direction and determined the ship's whereabouts.

The steward and cook sat together in the galley smoking their pipes, and those sailors not on duty took that time to relax, smoking, singing, playing cards, and telling long, improbable stories, often referred to as yarns.

At 8:00 P.M., the second mate struck eight bells. The captain entered his calculations about direction and location in the ship's record, or log book, and the first mate set up the watch schedule. The helmsman (the sailor steering the ship) changed shifts, and the cook shut the galley for the night. Finally, off-duty crew members went below to the forecastle to sleep.

right wrist and ankle of one to the left wrist and ankle of another, on a rough wooden deck built especially for transporting them. Between 250 and 450 captives—although sometimes as many as 700 to 800—were jammed together in this small, poorly ventilated space, which was about five feet high. Taller slaves were placed in the widest part of the ship; shorter slaves were positioned in narrower parts. As one former captive later explained, "The place in which we were confined was so full that no one could lie down; and we were obliged to sit all the time, for the room was not high enough for us to stand. . . . When we arrived at Charleston, I was not able to stand. It was more than a week after I left the ship before I could straighten my limbs."[74]

Eighteenth-century slave ship captain John Newton described the way slaves were crammed into slave quarters. Slaves were packed on ledges, he attests, "in two rows one above the other, on each side of the ship, close to each other, like books upon a shelf. I have known them so close that the shelf would not easily contain one more. And I have known a white man sent down among the men to lay them in these rows to the greatest advantage so that as little space as possible be lost."[75]

The atmosphere of these slave decks proved intolerable for both slaves and crew members. The space was so small and crammed with people that there was no room to move and no fresh air to breath. There was no bathroom, so people lay in their own filth, and because the conditions were so poor, sickness spread quickly. The disgusting smell alone made people sick to their stomachs. Some Africans went crazy, moaning and raving; others lost their will to live and died.

Slave ship captain James Barbot described how slave-quarter conditions even prevented

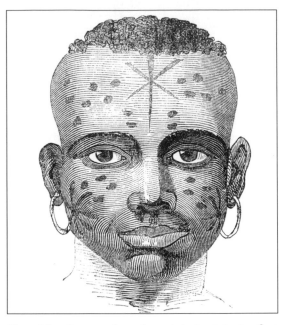

Slaves' heads were shaved to minimize injuries that could occur during fights. Here, a drawing shows what a slave might look like before being shaved.

the ship doctor from examining and treating ailing captives: "To administer proper remedies . . . between decks" was impossible to do "leisurely . . . because of the great heat that is there continually which is sometimes so excessive that the surgeons would faint away and the candles would not burn."[76]

Sleeping Arrangements

Arranging the captives in the slave decks each evening at sundown required the efforts of both the second mate and the boatswain, who went below, armed with a whip, to cram hundreds of people into the dank filthy hold. Most slaves slept on the bare boards of the slave ledges, but some Portuguese slavers provided coarse mats to lie on.

To maintain order during the night, the sailors appointed a monitor, one for every ten slaves. The monitor was usually a slave himself, who was given a cat-o'-nine-tails and was instructed to flog any slave who made noise or a disturbance. As Captain Thomas Phillips reported, "We have some thirty or forty Gold Coast negroes . . . to make guardians and overseers of their Whydah [Ouidah] negroes, and sleep among them to keep them from quarreling."[77] As a reward for their assistance, the monitors were provided with an old shirt and a pair of trousers, distinguishing them from the other slaves who were naked.

Even the threat of a monitor's whip could not prevent the battles for sleeping space that raged nightly in the slave hold. To minimize injuries, the ship's barber cut the fingernails and shaved their heads. During their nightly imprisonment in the slave deck, slaves were supposed to use buckets, placed in each sleeping area, as latrines. However, shackled as they were and with minimal space to move, it was often an impossible struggle to reach these buckets in the middle of the night.

One seventeenth-century slave trader from Portugal described arranging slaves in the hold and their terrible experience trying to survive:

Women who were pregnant were assembled in the back cabin, the children were huddled together . . . as if they were herrings in a barrel. If anyone wanted to sleep, they lay on top of each other. To satisfy their natural needs, they had bilge places . . . over the edge of the sea, but, as many feared to lose their place . . . they relieved themselves where they were, above all the men [who were] cruely pushed together, in such a way that the heat and the smell became intolerable.[78]

Feeding the Slaves

In his autobiography *The Interesting Narrative of the Life of Olaudah Equiano,* Equiano remembered the cruel treatment he received when sickness and sadness prevented him from eating.

"I became so sick and low that I was not able to eat, nor had I the least desire to taste anything. I now wished for the last friend, death, to relieve me; but soon, to my grief, two of the white men offered me eatables; and on my refusing to eat, one of them held me fast by the hands, and laid me across, I think, the windlass, and tied my feet, while the other flogged me severely."

Yet at the same time that the captives were forced to eat and were savagely pun-ished if they refused, they were also denied food they found palatable.

"One day [the whites] had taken a number of fishes; and when they had killed and satisfied themselves with as many as they thought fit, to our astonishment who were on deck, rather than give any of them to us to eat, as we expected, they tossed the remaining fish into the sea again, although we begged and prayed for some as well as we could, but in vain; and some of my countrymen, being pressed by hunger, took an opportunity, when they thought no one saw them, of trying to get a little privately; but they were discovered, and the attempt procured them some very severe floggings."

Slaves were kept in a state of constant hunger and were whipped for attempting to steal extra food.

The Daily Routine of the Captives

Generally, in mild weather slaves were brought above deck for air at eight o'clock in the morning. There, the ship's doctor would examine them for any sores and ailments. If they were ill, they were taken to a separate part of the ship for treatment. However, according to surgeon Alexander Falconbridge, sick slaves often endured further misery in their quarantined area:

The place allotted for the sick Negroes is under the half deck, where they lie on the bare planks. By this means those who are emaciated frequently have their skin and even their flesh entirely rubbed off, by the motion of the ship, from the prominent parts of the shoulders, elbows and hips so as to render the bones quite bare.[79]

If they were well, the slaves remained on deck and were given saltwater to wash themselves and palm oil to massage into their skin. As part of the morning routine, petty officers also examined the slaves' shackles to make sure they were secure.

Sometimes, after checking the iron shackles for any weaknesses, captains unlocked them because they knew that slaves survived the transatlantic crossing in better health and greater numbers if freed of irons. Most captains, however, so feared rebellion that they kept the male captives chained together, fastened to a thick iron ring bolted in the deck. Historians Daniel P. Mannix and Malcolm Cowley explain the general routine:

"If the weather was clear, [the slaves] were brought on deck . . . in the morning. The men were attached by their leg irons to the great chain that ran along the bulwarks on both sides of the ship; the women and half-grown boys were allowed to wander at will."[80]

To occupy the female captives, some slavers gave them colored beads. In agreeable weather, these women strung beads to pass the time on deck. At six in the evening, the men were chained and confined to the slave quarters below. Women and children were permitted to remain above deck longer, and sometimes they were allowed to sleep on deck.

Feeding the Captives

Slaves were fed twice a day at ten in the morning and four in the afternoon. They ate in groups on deck in good weather. In rough weather though, they ate in the hold.

During the voyage, slaves were fed small rations of food, in part because slavers were continually fearful of running out of rations before reaching land. As a result, the slaves suffered from great hunger. Olaudah Equiano remembered the cruel flogging some captives received aboard ship when they first begged for and then tried to steal extra food.

A sailor climbs the ratlines, ropes that provided footholds while ascending the rigging.

Lack of air circulating in the slave decks caused many slaves to suffocate. Alexander Falconbridge, a slave ship surgeon whose remarks have been excerpted from Thomas Howard's *Black Voyage,* left a particularly clear picture of the slave hold. When bad weather confined all of the captives below deck, they were chained together in their cramped slave ledges.

"Fevers among the negroes ensued. While they were in this situation, my profession requiring it, I frequently went down among them, till at length their apartments became so extremely hot as to be only sufferable for a very short time. But the excessive heat was not the only thing that rendered their situation intolerable. The deck, that is the floor of their rooms, was so covered with the blood and mucous . . . that it resembled a slaughter-house. It is not in the power of the human imagination to picture to itself a situation more dreadful or disgusting."

In his autobiography, entitled *The Interesting Narrative of the Life of Olaudah Equiano,* Equiano also remembered the slave deck and how it felt to be chained in the hold.

"The stench of the hold was so intolerably loathsome, that it was dangerous to remain there for any time. . . . [When] the whole ship's cargo were confined together, it became absolutely pestilential. The closeness of the place, and the heat . . . added to the number in the ship, which was so crowded that each had scarcely room to turn himself, [and] almost suffocated us. This . . . brought on a sickness among the slaves, of which many died. . . . [The] wretched situation was again aggravated by the galling of the chains, now . . . insupportable, and the filth of the necessary tubs, into which the children often fell, and were almost suffocated."

As a way to restrain the captives' ravenous appetite and make them eat more slowly, slavers sometimes used a monitor, according to one historian, to signal when the slaves were allowed to scoop up their food with their fingers or wooden spoon and when they were allowed to swallow what they were chewing. Monitors also watched closely for slaves who refused to eat. Many slaves tried to starve themselves, and if the monitor caught them, the captives were whipped.

Because starved captives hold little monetary value, torturous methods were used to force them to eat. "Upon the Negroes refusing to take sustenance," reported Alexander Falconbridge, "I have seen coals of fire, glowing hot, put on a shovel and placed so near their lips to scorch and burn them."[81] Crew members also used a particularly cruel device called a speculum orum, which pried open the mouth of a slave to allow force-feeding.

Dancing the Slaves

Slavers also believed that forcing slaves to sing and dance once a day was a necessary part of the Middle Passage. Thomas Trotter, a surgeon on board the *Brookes* in 1783, observed, "Those who were in irons were ordered to stand up and make what motions they could, leaving a passage for such as were out of irons to dance around the deck."[82]

Traders maintained that this exercise regime kept the slaves in good condition throughout the journey. However Ecroyde Claxton, a doctor aboard the *Young Hero,* revealed the truth about dancing the slaves. He said, "They sing, but not for their amusement. The captain ordered them to sing, and they sang songs of sorrow. Their sickness, fear of being beaten, their hunger, and the memory of their country."[83]

If a slave refused to dance or seemed sluggish in his movements, crew members whipped him with a cat-o'-nine-tails. Reported slaver Richard Drake, "We had half the gang on deck today for exercise; they danced and sang, under the driver's whip, but are far from sprightly."[84] Generally slaves remained in their irons and were forced to move in any way they were able. Captives used a drum, the bottom of a tub, or an African banjo to make music. Sometimes a sailor might play the bagpipes or fiddle as accompaniment.

The Daily Routine of the Crew

The grueling and complex routine of sailing a slave ship or any merchant ship across the Atlantic Ocean during the eighteenth and nineteenth centuries was an endless task. The twenty-four-hour-a-day schedule, called the watch, was divided into six four-hour shifts, manned by a handful of men, each responsible for a vast number of chores. While the captain charted the ship's course and petty officers made sure the captain's orders were carried through, sailors concentrated on two areas of work: manipulating the ropes, or rigging, and working the sails.

Rigging supported and controlled the sails, masts, and yards. There were two types of rigging, and sailors worked with both: standing rigging, which remained in place and did not move, and running rigging, which could be hauled in or let out, tightened, wound around a winch (crank), or uncoiled.

The other demanding aspect of a sailor's duty on board a slave ship involved working the sails. Seamen moved the sails, adjusting their angles and increasing or reducing them by manipulating the rigging. Following the officers' instructions, seamen pulled the special rigging, or sheets, to extend a sail and the halyards to raise or lower it.

Sailors could accomplish much of the work from the deck, where they were able to pull or let out the appropriate rope. However, frequently sailors climbed aloft using the specially fashioned rigging called ratlines to gain their footing.

Caring for the sails and rigging was part of taking care of the ship itself. Sailors tarred the masts and the cracks in the hold; greased the windlass (a machine used to haul in the ship's anchor); scrubbed, painted, oiled, and varnished the deck; not to mention scraped rust from all metal parts, including chains, anchors, and guns.

One of the most exhausting jobs for seamen, however, involved pumping bilge water. Two to seven sailors united in the backbreaking work of pulling large levers to suction the excess water out of the hold and up onto the deck where it flowed out the side openings, called scuppers. Pumping water caused deadening fatigue, and the strain pushed some crews to desert or mutiny. As a result the carpenter who managed to plug leaks and keep the ship watertight earned the praise of every man on board.

The Rhythm of Work

Two qualities stand out to describe work at sea. One, it was collective. Men worked together and depended on each other to do a good job, so that one man might easily take up a task where another left off. If, for example, a seaman were mending a sail and had to stop in the middle because his shift during the watch was over, he would have to leave his work in such a way that the new sailors might easily continue and finish mending the torn sail.

Also men relied on each other to keep the ship safe. A well-tarred hull, watertight and dry, would benefit all because leaks could endanger everyone.

The other unique aspect of life at sea was that work was done in public. Everyone could see what others were doing. Experienced sailors knew how to perform the basic tasks and had seen others perform them, from the captain's work on down. "Consequently," asserts historian W. Jeffrey Bolster, "even the lowest ordinary seaman considered himself a judge of his officers . . . and there was considerable pressure to demonstrate one's skills."[85] It was virtually impossible to hide a job badly done because other crew members closely watched each task as a sailor did it. Sometimes seamen exposed the inadequacies of their superior officers by following their incorrect orders to the greatest detail.

Sailor's Slang and Sea Chants

The way seamen talked to one another revealed the unique way they related to each other. Sailors primarily communicated with short, clear commands. Each sentence or phrase had a specific meaning everyone immediately understood and obeyed. Sailors were particularly inventive when describing punishment. The phrase "the cat wailed on 'market day'" meant to flog someone, and a seaman severely punished was "dried out in the shrouds."[86]

Spirits and Cannibals

For some slaves, ship life seemed so foreign that they believed they had entered a world of demon spirits. In his autobiography *The Interesting Narrative of the Life of Olaudah Equiano*, Equiano mentioned aspects of his voyage that he could explain only by the supernatural.

"During our passage, I first saw flying fishes, which surprised me very much; . . . I also now first saw the use of the quadrant [an instrument to measure altitude]; I had often with astonishment seen the mariners make observations with it. . . . One of them . . . made me one day look through it. The clouds appeared to me to be land, which disappeared as they passed along. This heightened my wonder; and I was now more persuaded than ever, that I was in another world, and that every thing about me was magic."

One great fear slaves had centered around the uncertainty of their future. Upon leaving Africa, slavers often explained to the captives that they were being taken across the sea to farm and work the land. No matter how many times the crew tried to persuade them of this, however, many captives feared that the white men were cannibals and that the unfortunate Africans would soon be eaten.

As Equiano explains, "We thought we should be eaten by these ugly men [the white planters and merchants who came aboard when Olaudah's slave ship first arrived in Barbados]. . . . There was much dread and trembling among us . . . that at last the white people got some old slaves [who] . . . told us we were not to be eaten but to work."

Throughout the Middle Passage, slaves not only endured terrible conditions but also lived in fear of what was to come.

Cursing was another characteristic way seamen spoke to each other. From captain to cabin boy, everyone cursed, sometimes jokingly, sometimes seriously. The eighteenth-century clergyman George Whitefield wondered whether seamen could "pull their ropes without swearing."[87] As a joke or in earnest, asserts Marcus Rediker, "seamen damned each other's blood, cursed each other's bodies and wished misery and destruction on their foes. Seamen hurled insults at each other and at their officers: [they yelled] You fat-gutted chucklehead! Blood and thunder, you . . . knave!"[88]

Using Slaves on Board

Tropical diseases and other hardships sometimes killed or disabled so many crew members that slave ship captains required the captives to work on board. While they worked, officers forced the slaves to sing, no matter what the job. Singing was supposed to keep up the spirit of the slaves. Some historians believe that the rhythmic way sailors sing as they pull rigging or push the crank of a windlass came from watching African slaves working together aboard a ship.

Female slaves helped the cook with tasks such as grinding corn. Male slaves were often used to help sailors with particularly unpleasant jobs. "Last Tuesday," wrote Richard Drake, "the smallpox began to rage, and we hauled 60 corpses out of the hold. . . . We stimulated the blacks with rum in order to get their help in removing corpses."[89]

Keeping the slave decks clean was another job some slavers considered particularly important, and they frequently used the slaves who slept there to help maintain the areas. Captain Thomas Phillips even appointed some captives as overseers, providing them with whips: "[To] make [the] negroes scrape the decks where they lodge . . . to [avoid any illness] that may engender from filth and dirtiness; when we appoint a guardian we give him a cat o' nine tails as a badge of his office."[90]

Inner Fortitude

Whether because slaves refused to eat or as way to coerce them to clean the slave decks, slavers whipped, flogged, and cruelly mistreated the captives. As former slave Louis Asa-Asa remembers in his memoir, published in 1831, "The slaves we saw on board were chained together by the legs below deck, so close they could not move. They were flogged very cruelly; I saw one of them flogged till he died; we could not tell what for."[91]

Afloat in the middle of the ocean and subjected to routines they neither chose nor understood, captives were miserable and confused aboard the ship. Olaudah Equiano wondered how European seamen were even able to move the ship in the water. Along with other slaves, locked in the hold and manacled to each other, Equiano surmised that the sailors were demons who performed magic with wind, cloth, and ropes to guide the vessel across the great expanse.

The whole experience so terrified Equiano that he later wrote, "I even wished [I remained a slave in Africa] in preference to my present situation which was filled with horrors of every kind, still heightened by my ignorance of what I was to undergo."[92] Despite his fear and horror, Equiano endured, like so many Africans, who managed to survive the Middle Passage.

Surviving the Journey

As the slave ship made its way across the Atlantic Ocean, life was a continual battle for survival for both slaves and crew members. At any moment the terrible daily hardships could easily overwhelm and destroy everyone on board.

For the slaves, chained and imprisoned in the putrid hold, surviving the suffocating slave deck and the deadly diseases it bred became a feat of endurance. Another equally threatening aspect of daily life involved the abuse and mistreatment that slavers inflicted on captives during the crossing. As freed slave Ottobah Cugoano later expressed, "It would be needless to give a description of all the horrible scenes which we saw, and base [degrading] treatment which we met with in this dreadful captive situation."[93]

For the crew, life aboard a slave ship was also extremely perilous. Like the slaves, crew members died of the contagious diseases that ravaged the hold, and slave ship captains treated crew members cruelly, often punishing them severely for petty blunders. Many sailors could recount stories such as the one seaman James Morley remembered: For accidentally breaking a glass belonging the captain, "I was tied up to the tiller in the cabin by my hands, and then flogged with a cat [-o'-nine-tails], and kept hanging there some time."[94]

Other perils also challenged those aboard the ship. The unpredictability of the weather and the imprecise navigation skills of the era made crossing the Atlantic Ocean dangerous. Crew members often wrestled with ropes and sails as wind and driving rain pummeled their tiny vessels. In addition, slave ships might find themselves embroiled in a battle at sea with a pirate ship or a vessel from a rival nation. Often without warning, in the middle of the Atlantic the captives and crew would suddenly become the target of cannon fire from an attacking ship.

Abuse and Mistreatment of the Captives

The dangers captives suffered from outside forces such as bad weather and enemy ships were far less life-threatening than the cruelty and wanton acts of violence they had to endure on board. From the moment they were captured, slaves were abused and mistreated. The violence they experienced on land in Africa continued and was often heightened during the Middle Passage. As former slave Olaudah Equiano comments, "The white people looked and acted . . . in so savage a manner. . . . I had never seen such instances of brutal cruelty."[95]

Sometimes, historians attest, slave treatment was less vicious than other times, depending on the nature of the captain and the crew. But even sympathetic behavior during the eighteenth century could include very brutal actions. African women, for example, were regularly abused by the slave ship crew.

Slaver John Newton, known as a kind captain, noted one practice in his journal: "When

Storms and rough weather were just a few of the dangers that threatened slave ships on their journeys.

women and girls are taken on aboard a ship, naked, trembling, terrified, perhaps almost exhausted from cold, fatigue and hunger, they are often exposed to the wanton rudeness of white savages."[96] Women who protested were whipped and beaten.

Some slave trading companies such as the Dutch Middleburg Commercial Company, active during the eighteenth century, made it illegal and severely punishable for sailors to assault female slaves. On the long, exhausting trip to and from Africa, however, where crew members were themselves often brutalized, it is unlikely the laws were enforced.

Captain Newton tried to protect female slaves on his ship. Once, when he caught a sailor assaulting an African woman, he wrote that he "put him in irons. I hope this has been the first affair of the kind on board and I am determined to keep [the crew] quiet if possible. If anything happens to the woman, I shall impute it to him."[97]

At the same time that African women became targets of abuse from the white crew members, they were also given more freedom than men. Male slaves were kept in irons for longer periods throughout the voyage. They also spent a greater amount of time in the hold and were forced to do more strenuous labor aboard the ship. Women and children were often allowed to remain on deck without shackles throughout the voyage.

Sickness and Death

In addition to the physical abuse slaves suffered, they also often fell victim to any number of fatal epidemics, such as smallpox, that the unsanitary conditions of slave ship life bred. Keeping the slaves healthy became a major worry for slavers during the Middle Passage. As a way of preventing widespread illness, some crews tried to keep the slave decks clean. "Thrice a week," reported slaver Jean Barbot, "we perfume betwixt' decks with a quantity of good vinegar in pails, and red hot bullets in them to expel the bad air, after the place had been well scrubbed with brooms: after which the deck is cleaned with cold vinegar."[98]

However, not all slave ship captains attempted to maintain a degree of cleanliness to promote health. Eyewitness accounts such as the one left by slaver Richard Drake, who was a trader for twenty-four years, describe a different scene below deck: "On the eighth day [out at sea] . . . I took my round of the half deck, holding a camphor bag in my teeth; for the stench was hideous. The sick and dying were chained together. I saw pregnant women give birth of babies whilst chained to

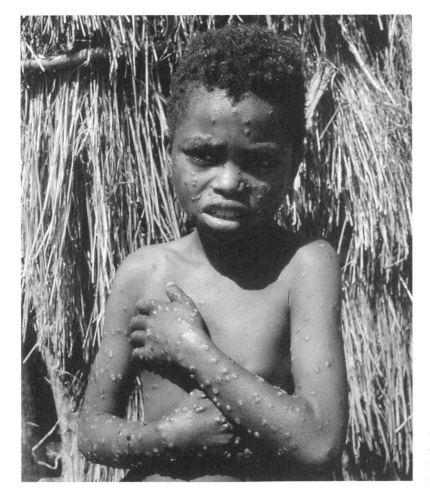

A modern photo of an African boy with smallpox, one of the diseases rampant on slave ships.

Emergencies at Sea

On February 29, 1758, Captain Joseph Harrison of the *Rainbow* wrote to his ship's owners, informing them of his situation. The following portion of his letter, excepted from *Black Cargoes*, by Daniel P. Mannix and Malcolm Cowley, illustrates the dangers a slave ship captain had to face as he made his slaving voyage.

"We arrived here on the 25 [February] in company with Capt. Perkins from Bonny, and Capt. Forde from Angola. . . . I expected to sail for hence for South Carolina in five days, having on board 225 slaves, all in good health except eight. On the 23rd of June last, I had the misfortune to fall in with a French brig privateer [enemy ship], of fourteen 6-ponders [cannons]. We engaged him four hours, and were so near . . . that I expected every moment we should run on board him, as he had shot away all my running rigging and the fluke of my small bow anchor. My standing rigging and sails were mostly cut to pieces and the privateer was in a little better condition. Fifteen of his shot went through and through my sides. I lost in my engagement my boatswain. . . . My first and second mates, three landsmen, and one servant wounded. The privateer being well satisfied sheered off. We were three days in repairing."

corpses, which our drunken overseers had not removed."[99]

Often, unsanitary conditions, combined with inadequate food rations, caused raging epidemics of fever, the flux, and smallpox to sweep through the slave decks and kill many of the captives. Venture Smith, an African slave who was later freed, recalled that at the time of his crossing, there was "a great mortality by the small pox, which broke out on board. . . . Out of the two hundred and sixty that sailed from Africa, [we found] not more than two hundred alive."[100]

Slaves whom the captain believed were too weak and sick to recover, were sometimes hurled into the ocean. Some slavers believed ridding the ship of diseased slaves might stop contagion from spreading. As Thomas Howard explains, "Ruthless ship captains would throw over the side the first slave or two to show any evidence of sickness, thus hoping to prevent its spread."[101]

When slaves and crew members died, their bodies were also tossed into the sea. Often a school of sharks followed the slave ship to feed on the bodies thrown overboard.

The Perils of Maritime Work

In addition to the constant danger of becoming deathly ill, seamen faced the ongoing hazards of maritime work itself. Seamen often became maimed or disabled as a result of the everyday chores. Even loading and unloading barrels of goods for trade could cause injury, particularly since heavy crates sliding around the hold of a rocking ship could crush a sailor's limb. "It was not unusual," one sailor reported, "for a finger to be lost to a rolling case, for an arm or leg to be broken by shifting cargo, or for a hand to be burned in tarring ropes."[102]

Sometimes seamen died while working on the ship. For example, during a strong wind or turbulent sea, crew members perched on a rope rung high above the deck could lose their balance, fall overboard, and drown. Also, the equipment used aboard a slave ship was heavy. If, as a result of the wear

Life on an African Slave Ship

and tear of life at sea, a loose iron spike or piece of equipment fell from a yard and hit a crew member below, the blow could kill him.

As historian Marcus Rediker notes, "The chances of a seaman ending his life in . . . a catastrophe were high, and many a man fell from the rigging, was washed overboard, or was fatally struck by falling gear."[103]

Attacking Ships

Another peril that crews suffered was the ongoing possibility of a hostile attack from an enemy ship. These vessels might be manned by pirates, privateers, or coastal raiders cruising the waters for plunder. Attacks were frequent, and the slave ports in the Caribbean were particularly treacherous for any trading ship bound for the West Indies.

Newspapers at the time often ran articles about slavers narrowly escaping pirate attacks. On October 3, 1754, the *South Carolina Gazette,* for example, reported that "Capt. Seymour, in a large Bemuda Sloop . . . had been chased . . . for two Days and Nights by a large Black Schooner, [later] being informed [that] she was a Pirate."[104]

Slave ships faced attacks by pirates, who stole the crew's money and possessions as well as the ship's cargo and supplies.

Articles told of ships that pirates had robbed. In the same issue of the *South Carolina Gazette,* a story about a sloop captained by James Berry recounts how the vessel was

boarded by a fine large Bermuda built sloop, arm'd only with Blun de busses [guns], commanded by a Spaniard (who

said he had taken many Prizes on this Coast . . .) with a mixed crew of many Nations [who] strip[ed] Capt. Berry, a Passenger he had, and his Crew, of all their Cloaths [clothes], Money, Watches, &c, and took out of the Vessel, two negro men, 4 Hogsheads of Rum, one of Sugar, with whatever else they wanted.[105]

In addition to the dangers that pirate attacks posed, a slave ship might discover itself caught between the crossfire of warring nations. Over the four hundreds years during which European nations participated in the slave trade, alliances shifted frequently, and even if not actively at war, each European nation defended its own territorial waterways. If, for example, an English slaver happened to drift into Spanish territory as it made its way across the Atlantic, the seamen aboard might find themselves in the midst of a pitched battle at sea, fighting for their lives.

Sailors understood the risks of these battles, which could often leave them badly wounded or maimed. Sometimes, they banded together in protest. "[We] did not hire [ourselves] to fight," seamen Samuel Howell asserted in 1713. "Who would maintain [us] and [our] Familys in case (we) should lose a Legg or an Arm?"[106] At best, after years at sea, if they were still alive, they emerged from the experience broken, sickly, and unfit to work.

Discipline and Abuse of the Crew

Although pirate attacks were brutal, they were rare, and some historians believe that the most perilous aspect of manning a slave ship was the cruel discipline a captain or another commanding officer used to intimidate the crew. Seamen were regularly beaten for minor infractions or

Crew Conditions

Crew conditions aboard a slave ship caused significant illness and a notable number of deaths. Although more than half of all crew deaths occurred on the African coast, during the Middle Passage, sailors suffered from conditions similar to those suffered by slaves, including exposure to disease, insufficient food, and deprivation when the voyage took a long time.

In his book *Stand the Storm,* historian Edward Reynolds describes the treatment of sailors during the Middle Passage.

"Day and night, seamen were exposed to wind and sea. They were forced to sleep on deck [especially when the ship was overcrowded] exposed to all types of weather, an old tarpaulin thrown over a boom being their only shelter. This exposure frequently caused illness and death. . . . Often, the crew was given only one meal a day [consisting of a small amount of bread, meat, and water] and because they were the first to be deprived when there was a shortage of provisions, it was common for sailors to beg rations from the slaves. Provisions were commonly refused to sick sailors: on many slavers, the rule was 'no work, no victuals.'"

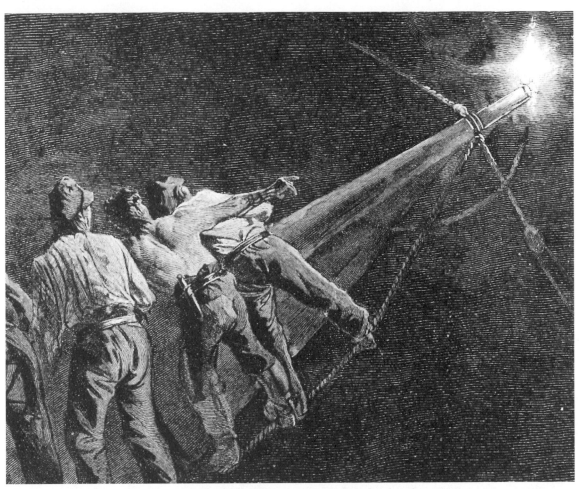

As lightning strikes the bowsprit, sailors work together to protect the ship from the ravages of a storm.

occurrences. The cook, for example, might become the target of a captain's murderous rage if the captain disliked how the food tasted. Once, when the cook on a particular slave ship served tainted meat, the infuriated captain beat both the cook and steward and tied them together. They were imprisoned in the hold for two days.

Officers often beat crew members to punish and discipline them. As a result, sailors sustained lasting injuries, including lameness or constant headaches, or even permanent bouts of dizziness. Sometimes bouts of dizziness were referred to as "falling sickness." Ordinary seaman John Marchant reported before the High Court of Admiralty that he had been caned mercilessly by first mate John Yates during one voyage. Because of the caning, he became continually "troubled with a diziness in his Head . . . in so much that he cannot go aloft without danger of falling down."[107]

Even captives such as Olaudah Equiano expressed horror over the brutality officers showed crew members during the Middle Passage. Describing his feelings in his memoir, he remarked,

Violent weather threatened the lives of both the crew, who fought to get the ship through the storm, and the slaves locked in the hold.

I had never seen among any people such instances of brutal cruelty; and this not only shown towards us blacks, but also to some of the whites themselves. One white man in particular I saw, when we were permitted to be on deck, flogged so unmercifully with a large rope near the foremast, that he died in consequence of it; and they tossed him over the side as they would have done a brute.[108]

Relations Among the Crew

It is little wonder that crew relations were tense. Sailors on a slave ship lived for months at a time in the middle of the ocean on a ship that most teenagers could cross in fifteen paces. They slept in hammocks for only three or four hours at a time in a forecastle that stank of bilge water, and they rarely had enough to eat or drink. They always felt chilled or wet and lived day after day in the same damp clothes, sharing the small cramped space of the boat with fifteen to forty-five other people.

The type of people who frequently manned slave ships heightened the harsh environment: poor vagrants or runaways, drunkards, hardened seamen, and tyrannical captains. One justification officers gave for their inhuman treatment of seamen was that severe discipline provided order within an otherwise unruly group.

However, cut off from contact with other people, sailors created a bond with each other, forged from the years spent together aboard ship. Pitted against the forces of nature, seamen banded together to battle the ever-present dangers of wind and water.

Sailors also became allies to unite against the power and cruelty of commanding officers. Within the ship's world, two separate communities arose—seamen at the bottom of the social ladder and officers at the top, each group socializing among themselves. Sometimes stronger seamen looked out for the welfare of weaker seamen. For example, "young seamen often tried to protect the older ones by giving them more or better provisions or by shielding them from an abusive captain." In 1749 it was reported that when a drunken captain, Thomas Sanderson, hit the boatswain aboard his ship, "the Crew rose and said that [the Captain] should not beat the Boatswain (who was a very old man.)"[109]

Racial Relations on Board

Another aspect of crew relations involved the relationship between black and white mariners. As historian W. Jeffrey Bolster explains, "One of the most significant changes during the period between 1740 and 1820 was in the increase in the number of black mariners who manned ships traveling the Triangle of Trade."[110] Most men were slaves, rented out by their masters to assist on trading voyages. Some, however, were free men, who saw seafaring as one of their only opportunities to make a living.

Blacks attained skills that enabled them to serve in any station aboard ship, but prejudice denied them positions beyond that of able-bodied seamen. Usually, free blacks were hired as cabin boys, cooks, musicians, and stewards. However, slaves who worked on board might be allowed to assume positions of authority more easily than free blacks. Slaves could serve their white masters, using the very seafaring skills with which free blacks were not allowed to use to earn a living.

Racial prejudice also included ongoing brutal physical abuse. In his autobiography, John Jea, a veteran seacook during the early nineteenth century, recalled enduring terrible treatment because of his color. "They used to flog, beat, and kick me about the same as if I had been a dog,"[111] he recounted. Yet Jea persisted for years because seafaring allowed him to make a living, travel widely, and, as a preacher, spread the word of spiritual awakening and social equality, two ideas that ultimately contributed greatly to outlawing the slave trade.

Opthamalia

One of the worst diseases that slaves and crew could acquire during the voyage across the Atlantic was a blinding eye infection called opthamalia. In his book *Black Voyage*, Thomas Howard quotes from the letter of J. B. Romaigne, a twelve-year-old boy on his way to visit his father in the West Indies. Romaigne's letter tells what happened as a result of an opthamalia outbreak on the French slaver *Le Rodeur*.

"The man who preserved his sight the longest recovered the soonest. To his exertions alone . . . is it owing that we are now within a few leagues of Guadaloupe, this twenty-second day of June, 1819. . . . I am myself almost well. . . . Among the slaves 39 are completely blind. . . . This morning the Captain called all hands on deck. . . . The mate picked out thirty nine who were completely blind, and, with the assistance of the rest of the crew, tied a piece of ballast to the legs of each. The miserable wretches were then thrown into the sea."

Racial relations on board were not always horrible, though. Olaudah Equiano, for example, described one rare instance when a friendship formed between blacks and whites aboard ship. As a young teenager enslaved on his master's ship, Equiano wrote that he met

> a young lad who had never been at sea before, about four or five years older than myself; his name was Richard Baker. . . . Soon after I went on board, he showed me a great deal of . . . attention. . . . [F]or the space of two years [he] was my constant companion and instructor. Although he had many slaves of his own, . . . such a friendship was cemented between us . . . a faithful friend who, at the age of fifteen, discovered a mind superior to prejudice.[112]

Surviving Storms

In addition to the harsh treatment sailors received at the hands of their superiors, they also had to grapple with harsh weather, which made slave ship life a life-and-death drama. Historian Marcus Rediker recounts the valiant efforts of two seamen, who tried to keep their ship from capsizing in the midst of a raging storm. While

> whitecapped waves slapped the bobbing ship and . . . water casks rolled from side to side . . . the violence of the elements . . . quickly flipped the frail vessel onto its side. . . . Two seamen armed with axes went on deck [to cut down the foretop mast and some of the rigging.] As they hacked [away], a monstrous wave hit the forward part of the ship, snapping the foremast as though it was a thin twig and carrying . . . one . . . sailor into the sea. . . .

The other seaman was crushed between the mast and the side of the ship.[113]

Devastating storms also brought death to the slaves. Sometimes disastrous weather might result in a path of destruction that claimed hundreds of lives. In 1702, for example, more than eight hundred slaves died when the Danish vessel the *KronPrintzen* perished during a tempest at sea.

Even if they survived the storm, the horror of the experience left slaves terrified and bewildered. Locked on the hold of the ship, they braved extreme anguish as the brutal weather tore the vessel apart. Sometimes, the captives were flung about the lurching ship so violently that they suffered broken bones. One Portuguese captain, who lived through a violent storm off the coast of Mozambique, left a vivid account:

> Suddenly, the weather closes in, and the sea rises so high and forcefully that the ships obey the waves without course or control, at the mercy of the winds. It is then that the din [noise] from the slaves, chained to one another, becomes horrible. The clanking of the irons, the moans, the weeping, the cries, the waves breaking over one side of the ship and then the other, the shouting of the sailors, the whistling of the winds, and the continuous roar of the waves. . . . Some of the food supplies are pushed overboard. . . . Many slaves break their legs and their arms, while others die of suffocation. One ship will break apart from the fury of the storm and sink. The other drifts on, dismasted, ruined by the force of the ocean . . . on the verge of capsizing.[114]

When mariners battled a tumultuous sea, they relied on slaves to help shoulder the

The remains of a wrecked ship. Slaves trapped below deck faced certain death if the ship sank.

burden. Captains used slaves to relieve tired crews of the backbreaking job of pumping water, often pushing them to the point of physical collapse. According to historian Hugh Thomas,

> Slaves were often called on to help an over worked or exhausted crew. Thus we hear how in the midst of these distresses, the vessels, after being three weeks at sea, became so extremely leaky, as to require constant exertion at the pumps. It was found necessary, therefore, to take some of the ablest negroes out of the irons and employ them at this labour, in which they were often worked beyond their strength.[115]

During storms, the captives on board were sometimes in danger of more than the weather. In 1738 a Dutch slaver foundered on rocks off the coast of South America. Stormy weather blinded the crew, and the ship was about to sink. Asserts Thomas, "The crew closed the hatches of the slave decks to avoid pandemonium and then escaped with fourteen slaves who had been helping them; 702 slaves were left to drown."[116]

Factors of Survival

During the slave trade, ship captains often argued over the most efficient way to transport slaves while minimizing disease and loss of life. Their interest derived from discovering how to make the highest profit. Says Thomas Howard, "Some captains favored giving each slave plenty of room, thus giving each and all a better chance for health en route." Other captains thought that filling the ship beyond capacity would ensure the greatest profit from the slaving voyage. Howard described their motto as "don't worry about the loss from disease, because those who survived would more than make up the cost of the dead."[117]

According to many historians today, however, the length of the voyage played a far more significant role than the number of slaves a ship carried. Slaves aboard a ship that took a little over three weeks (the least amount of time an eighteenth-century slaver required to sail from Africa to the New World) had a greater chance of survival than ships that took three months. According to historian Edward Reynolds, "The time-span of the voyage and the danger of . . . contagious disease probably had more effect on mortality than overcrowding. . . . The reduced rations sometimes necessary during long voyages lowered the resistance of both slaves and crew. . . . The longer the voyage the greater the chance of illness and death."[118]

Staying alive amid extreme abuse was the real concern for most Africans and crew members. Even though the slave traders mistreated the slaves profoundly, they had a great interest in keeping the enslaved Africans alive. As one slave trader observed, "There was no profit on a slaving voyage until the Negroes were landed alive and sold."[119]

 Resistance

Faced with the prospect of leaving Africa forever, Ottobah Cugoano, then in his early teens, devised a desperate plan along with other captives aboard a slave ship bound for the Americas. In his memoir, published in 1787, Cugoano writes: "A plan was concerted amongst us, that we might burn and blow up the ship, and to perish all together in the flames."[120]

Cugoano's plan called for the boys and women aboard to carry out the plot because the men were kept chained below in the slave deck. But the group was betrayed by one of the African women on board, and, as Cugoano explains, "the discovery was likewise a cruel and bloody scene."[121]

Given the brutal consequences of resistance and harsh conditions of slave ship life in general, it is remarkable that slaves found the courage to resist or that any rebellions were successful at all. The captives had many factors working against them. The lack of a common language made it difficult for them to unite. Often captives belonged to different tribes. The Wolofs, Fulani, Ashanti, and Mandingos each spoke their own distinct language, and sometimes they were political rivals.

In addition, the majority of the captives wore heavy chains throughout the Middle Passage making escape nearly impossible. And the harsh punishment that resisters received was a strong deterrent; slavers made a point of brutalizing rebellious captives in front of the other slaves to horrify them and discourage further mutinous attempts.

However, the Africans' fighting spirit prevailed, and resistance among slaves appeared in many ways. Suicide was one way that captives exerted their free will within the confines of a slave ship. Mutiny and violent rebellion were two others. Resistance occurred on ships from every slave trading nation, and even during the

Female slaves were unchained at times, but men endured virtually the entire voyage across the Atlantic in chains.

An accurate number of slave rebellions aboard ships is difficult to estimate since officers often kept such attempts private.

early days, captives showed a strong drive to regain their freedom.

The Number of Rebellions

Between 1699 and 1850, Lloyd's London Shipping List reported more than 150 attempts of slave mutinies. Some historians estimate one insurrection every eight to ten journeys. In all likelihood, the number was far greater, but an accurate account is difficult to calculate.

Surviving documents that might support a truer figure have yet to surface, and during the slave trading years, slave ship officers wanted to hide instances of rebellion. A captain who killed slaves to suppress a mutiny incurred a financial loss for his employers, the owners of the slave ship or trading company.

Losing money for investors lessened a captain's chances of receiving another expedition. He would rather blame the cause of death on slave illness than mar his reputation as a competent officer. Therefore, it was in his best interest simply to handle a rebellion without mentioning it in writing, unless the rebellion grew too large for him to cover up.

Successful Mutinies

In the majority of reported cases, crews crushed the rebellions, but from time to time captives did emerge victorious. One of the earliest successful uprisings occured in 1532 on the Portuguese slaver the *Misericordia*. The 109 slaves on board were being shipped from San Tome, an island off the Gold Coast of Africa, to Elmina, a Portuguese slave fort. Along the way a band of captives revolted against Captain Estevao Carreiro and his crew. The rebelling slaves killed all of their captors, except the pilot and two seamen, who escaped to Elmina in a longboat. Although there is no record of what happened to the ship or the slaves, historians believe that the ship was lost because, in most cases, slaves did not know how to navigate slavers.

Sometimes, however, survivors of a successful slave ship rebellion lived to tell their stories. For example, in 1742, while their ship lay moored in the Gambia River, slaves aboard the galley *Mary* wrested control from the captain and drove the ship ashore. The ship was plundered and destroyed by Africans who lived in the area, and during the violent struggle, most of the crew were killed. The captain and first mate were kept prisoners by the slaves on board for nearly a month. Finally, the two escaped and found shelter in a French fort on the Senegal River. The captain returned home to South Carolina, where the ship's owner, prominent Charleston merchant Samuel Wragg, awaited word of his slave cargo. Rumors of rebellion made their way across the ocean and were confirmed when, on October 24, 1743, the Charleston-based newspaper the *South Carolina Gazette* ran the following item: "One of Samuel Wragg's ships, the Mary, which delivered negro cargoes in Charleston in 1737, 1738, and 1739, was destroyed in the Gambia River in 1743."[122]

Sometimes rebellions took an unusual turn. Historian Hugh Thomas describes a mutiny in 1752 during which slaves on the *Marlborough* fought each other as well as their captors. As the ship left the slave trading post Bonny, located at the mouth of the Niger River in West Africa, about twenty-eight of the four hundred slaves on board were left unattended on deck. While the crew washed the slave decks below, the unattended slaves located some firearms. The slaves then attacked and shot most of the crew of 35 men.

The surviving sailors were commanded to sail back to Bonny, the home of many of the captives. Just off the African coast, however, the *Marlborough* was attacked again, this time by another British slaver, the *Hawk*. Again, the former captives fended off an enemy. However, in the melee, a skirmish erupted between Gold Coast Africans and those from Bonny. Accounts report that more than one hundred Africans died before the Gold Coasters won the standoff.

Joseph Cinque, the Mende slave who led the mutiny aboard the Spanish slave ship Amistad *in 1829.*

Other times, slaves were able to overtake a ship because of its small size and few crew members. Some historians point to the success of the rebellion aboard the schooner *Amistad* as an example. In 1839 Joseph Cinque, a West African slave, led a victorious uprising aboard this slaver, which was moored off the coast of Cuba. Had the *Amistad* been a 350-ton vessel, carrying a large crew of thirty men, many historians argue that the crew would have been able to subdue the captives.

Frequently, especially while still in Africa, illness and death decimated the ranks of European slavers. Once again, slaves took advantage of the depleted number of crew members left to guard them. In part because the ship still remained close to land, and in part because there were fewer sailors to overpower, slaves used the opportunity to plan an escape.

The Story of Tomba

Sometimes an individual's spirited and courageous attempts to free himself and others stand out from among the few surviving documents of slave resistance. Tomba, a particularly

---

The *Amistad*

In 1829 slaves on the Spanish sloop the *Amistad* rebelled and took command of the ship. Led by one of the enslaved Mende tribesman, Joseph Cinque, the slaves killed several crew members but spared the lives of two slave traders, Jose Ruiz and Pedro Montes, who promised to navigate the ship back to Africa.

Instead, Ruiz and Montes tricked the Africans and secretly headed west and north, hoping to strike land. After two months of zigzagging up the coast of North America, the schooner landed in Long Island, New York. The starved captives went ashore in search of provisions. Immediately, government officials seized them and took them to a prison in New Haven, Connecticut.

Once imprisoned, the captives of the *Amistad* found themselves in the middle of an international political battle between people who believed in slavery and abolitionists who argued against it.

The Spanish government and the crew members of the *Amistad* wanted the captives returned to them. As slavery advocates, they believed the Africans were property. Many Americans also argued on behalf of the slaveholders, although some thought that the Mende tribesmen should remain in the southern United States to work as slaves on plantations.

Abolitionists asserted that the Africans should be freed and allowed to remain in the United States as free men or to return to Africa. The case went all the way to the U.S. Supreme Court where a former U.S. president, John Quincy Adams, argued successfully on behalf of the captives.

Adams's winning argument centered around a question of legality, not human rights or morality. As a result of the 1807 laws that abolished transatlantic slave trading, the Court recognized that the captives had been taken unlawfully from Africa.

Under the protection of the American government, Cinque and the other enslaved Mende were free men once again. In 1832 several *Amistad* survivors, including Cinque, returned to Africa, where they settled in Liberia.

Insurrections were often unsuccessful because there were too many crew members for the slaves to overpower.

strong-willed leader, achieved fame because of his acts of rebellion in the holding barracoons of Sierra Leone and aboard the ship as it was being stocked with slaves. Before he was finally captured, Tomba led raids and killed many African and European slave traders.

John Atkins, a slave ship surgeon in the early 1700s, included Tomba's remarkable attempts in his 1753 memoir, *A Voyage to Guinea.* It was, however, the young rebel's attitude that first made an impression. Atkins writes:

As . . . Slaves are placed [in] Lodges near the Owner's House for . . . better viewing them, I had every day the Curiosity of Observing their Behavior, which with most of them was very dejected. Once . . . I could not help taking notice of one Fellow among the rest, of a tall strong make, and bold, stern aspect. As he imagined we were viewing them with a design to buy, he seemed to disdain his Fellow-Slaves for their Readiness to be examined, and . . . scorned looking at us, refusing to rise or stretch out his Limbs, as the [slave] Master commanded; [this] got him an unmerciful Whipping . . . which the Negro bore with Magnanimity, shrinking very little, and shedding a Tear or two, which he endavoured to hide as tho' ashamed. . . . All the company grew curious at his Courage. . . . [We were told] that this same Fellow, called Captain Tomba, was a Leader in some Country Villages that opposed [African slavers], and their Trade, at the River Nunes.[123]

Passive Resisters

Not all resistance involved violence and organized rebellion. Passive resisters, those who tried to oppose their captors without guns, also made an impact.

Jumping overboard was one common way of escaping captivity during the Middle Passage. Even during a mutiny, this choice was an option. As historian Selena Axelrod Wisnes relates,

In 1787, a cargo of slaves sailing from the Danish trading fort of Christianborg to Saint Croix attacked the ship's company with any weapon that came readily to hand, including shackles and chains that they had hammered off their legs. After a pitched battle that lasted over two hours, the crew finally retained control of the ship but not before 35 slaves sprang overboard into the sea.[124]

For the European slave trader, slave suicides generally meant one thing: loss of financial investment. In 1776 Captain Peleg Clarke wrote ship owner John Fletcher about a mass suicide:

I am sorry that I have so disagreeable a story now to tell which is [that], about the 8th of last month, our slaves rose on board and a large number of them jumped overboard, out of which twenty-eight men and two women were drowned. Six men were taken up by the Moree town people which

Security Measures

In his account of a voyage made in 1693 from England, excerpted in *Black Cargoes*, by Daniel P. Mannix and Malcolm Cowley, Thomas Phillips discusses measures he took to discourage slaves from rebellion.

"When our slaves are aboard we shackle the men two and two while we lie in port, and in sight of their own country, for 'tis then they attempt to make their escape, and mutiny; to prevent which we always keep [guards] upon the hatchways, and have a chest full of small arms, ready [loaded] and prim'd, constantly lying at hand upon the quarter-deck, together with some granada shells; and two of our quarter-deck guns, pointing on the deck then, and two more out of the steerage, the door of which is always kept shut, and well barr'd; they [the slaves] are fed twice a day; at 10 in the morning, and 4 in the evening, which is the time they are aptest to mutiny, being all upon deck; therefore all that time, [those] men . . . not employd in distributing their victuals to them . . . stand to their arms; [some men stand] with lighted matches at the great guns [loaded with ammunition and pointed] upon [the slaves] till they have done [eating] and gone down to their kennels between decks."

Mr. Klark, the [Dutch] governor of the fort at that place, took out of their hands, and has them in ounces [of gold] per head for taking them up, so I could not settle it with them, and being obliged to return to Accra again in order to settle, I have begged the favour of Mr. Mill [a member of one of the famous mercantile families of Guinea and the West Indies] to settle it for me.[125]

In 1790 Ecroyde Claxton, a ship's surgeon, described an experience with a slave who had thrown himself overboard and managed to escape: "The slave, 'perceiving that he was going to be caught, immediately dived under water and, by that means, made his escape, and came up again several yards from the vessel, and made signs it is impossible for me to describe in words, expressive of the happiness he had in escaping us.'"[126]

Refusing to eat was another way that slaves showed their resistance. Slavers watched captives closely to make sure all slaves ate their rations, and crew members used several means of forcing resisters to swallow food and drink water. If slaves refused, slavers sometimes beat them with pieces of rope until they gave in. Other times crew members used burning coals or a speculum to force-feed slaves. Reports Captain Theodore Canot, "It is the duty of a guard to report immediately whenever a slave refused to eat. . . . Negroes have sometimes been found in slavers who attempted voluntary starvation . . . his appetite is stimulated by the medical antidote of a [whipping]."[127]

Thwarted Rebellions

Usually, however, European slave crews overpowered rebellious captives, and punishment was drastic and especially brutal. Captain William Smith describes the methods used to kill one rebellious captive, who had tried to escape from the slave ship *Elizabeth* in 1727:

One of the two men negroes we had taken up along the ship-side . . . readily confessed he had kill'd the cooper with no other view but that he and his countrymen might escape undiscovered by swimming on shore. . . . We acquainted the negro that he was to die in an hour's time for murdering the white man. . . . the hour glass being run out, the murderer was carried onto the ship's forecastle, where he had a rope fastened under arms, in order to be hoisted up to the foreyard arm, to be shot to death. . . . Ten white men who were placed behind the barricade of the quarterdeck fired their musquets and instantly killed him. . . . The body being cut down upon the deck, the head was cut off and thrown overboard . . . for many of the blacks believe that, if they are put to death and not dismembered, they shall return again to their own country after they are thrown overboard.[129]

Because slave rebellions were so costly, slavers from rival European nations sometimes helped each other subdue rebelling captives. The Dutch slave ship captain Willem Bosman recounts how he and his men were able to quell a rebellion with the help of a French slaver and an English vessel anchored nearby. In this case, according to Bosman, the slaves

possessed themselves of a hammer; with which, in a short time, they broke all their fetters in pieces . . . after which they came

Slaves who were kept unchained sometimes took the opportunity to attack the crew and attempt to escape.

up on deck, and fell upon our men, some of whom they grievously wounded, and would certainly have mastered the ship if French and English vessels had not very fortunately happened to lie by us; who perceiving by our firing a distressed gun that something was in disorder aboard, immediately came to our assistance with chalops and men, and drove the slaves below deck. . . . Some twenty of them were killed.[129]

Captains who demanded that captives fill the positions of sick or disabled seamen sometimes found themselves caught up in a slave rebellion. In 1765 an article in the newspaper the *Newport Mercury* reported,

soon after [Captain Esek Hopkins and his ship, *Sally*] left the coast [of Africa], the number of his men being reduced by sickness, he was obliged to let some of the slaves to come upon deck to assist the people; these slaves contrived to get possession of the vessel; but was happily prevented by the captain, who killed, wounded, and forced overboard eighty of them which obliged the rest to submit.[130]

Other times, captives took advantage of the somewhat lax security during the period when traders were buying slaves. Because keeping slaves in the fetid hold of the ship bred diseases, which jeopardized the investment, captains often allowed the slaves to roam the decks. Although this practice reduced the outbreak of disease, it also sometimes invited rebellion. Captain Abijah Potter of the slave ship *Liberty*, for example, kept

the first six slaves he purchased unchained above deck. Their relative freedom gave the captives ample opportunity to escape. As historian Jay Coughtry explains, "While roaming around the main deck of the [ship] ironically named *Liberty,* unshackled and unguarded the slaves soon discovered an ax, and [killed the captain of the ship and a mate], before the rest of the crew reached the arms chest and subdued them."[131]

The Fear of Rebellion

Because slave revolts were such a problem, slave ship captains and merchant slave trading

Sailors kept a close watch for items that slaves could use as weapons, such as this piece of a broken cooking pot.

firms gave crew members explicit advice about how to avoid shipboard rebellions. In a letter from Captain John Fletcher to Captain Peleg Clarke, Fletcher advises, "Be very careful in keeping a good look out and watchful of your Negroes to prevent Insurrections."[132]

Heeding such warnings, captains employed many solutions to handle the rebellion problem. One of the most popular involved making sure that slaves came from different parts of Africa and had their own distinct languages and customs. That way, slaves were virtually unable to communicate with each other or easily plan an attack.

In his seafaring account, seventeenth century mariner Richard Simons describes the slaver's strategy of divide-and-conquer:

> The means used by those who trade to Guinea, to keep the Negroes quiet is to choose them from severall parts of ye Country, of different Langues; so that they find they cannot act joyntly, when they are not in a Capacity of Consulting one an other, and this they can not doe, in soe farr as they understand not one an other.[133]

As a result, rebellions were often individual attempts to gain freedom rather than planned group efforts. Rival tribes had a difficult time joining forces, and without a common language, it was nearly impossible to organize a powerful resistance.

Security Measures

Because shipboard rebellions were of such concern, captains often increased security measures to ensure a successful voyage. They kept captives in chains to control them and required a higher ratio of seamen to slaves.

They increased crew numbers so that there was one seaman for every ten to fifteen slaves. In addition, slavers constantly examined the decks for blunt or sharp objects that slaves might use as weapons.

As slave trader James Barbot wrote during his voyage in 1700,

> If care be not taken, [captives] will mutiny and destroy the ship's crew in hopes to get away. To prevent such misfortunes, we used to visit [the slaves] daily, narrowly searching every corner between decks, to see whether they have not found means, to gather any pieces of iron, or wood, or knives, about the ship, notwithstanding the great care we take not to leave any tools or nails, or other things in the way: which, however, cannot be always so exactly observ'd, where so many people are in the narrow compass of a ship.[134]

Each nation developed a reputation based on its success in controlling slave rebellions. The American slavers, especially those from Rhode Island, held the record for the fewest uprisings. "The mode of confining and securing Negroes in American slave ships . . . is abundantly more rigid than in British vessels,"[135] observed one eighteenth-century eyewitness.

Historians are unsure why Rhode Island's slave ships had the fewest mutinies since they often had relatively small crews. Some researchers suggest that using guns to quell revolts played a key role in the small number of rebellions aboard Rhode Island slavers. One witness aboard the slave ship *Nancy* later recounted how quickly Rhode Island crews relied on firearms to stop mutinies: "Four or five days after the voyage commenced, as the slaves were all together messing one day . . . one of them seized the master as he was pouring molasses into his victuals. . . . The master and crew then drove [the slaves] below with small arms, one . . . jumped overboard, and a few of the said slaves got slightly wounded."[136]

Researchers still do not know why resistance and rebellions occurred on some ships and not on others since there are no clear-cut, universal reasons for rebellion. It was not unusual, for example, to allow slaves to roam the deck of a ship during the early stages of the purchasing period, when there were only a few slaves on board. Crews at times allowed groups of as many as 160 slaves to spend the day above deck unchained. "A knowing trader will never use chains but when compelled, for the longer a slave is ironed the more he deteriorates," claimed slaver Theodore Canot, "and, as his sole object is to land a healthy cargo [for] pecuniary [monetary] interest."[137] Although it seems that rebellions should have been a problem during these moments of freedom, more often than not they weren't. Slaves simply took in the fresh air, and crews readied the ships for departure.

Although the valiant efforts of some enslaved rebel Africans did cause their deaths, their failed attempts only served to

Rebellious Crews

The gruesome conditions on slave ships also created tension between officers and crew members. In 1721, for example, second mate George Lowther aboard the *Gambia Castle,* a ship belonging to the Royal African Company, led a mutiny because he claimed the company had allowed the seamen's physical health to deteriorate drastically. In his book *Between the Devil and the Deep Blue Sea,* Marcus Rediker relates that "some difficulties apparently arose over procuring a cargo of slaves, and Lowther maintained that the merchants said that the seamen should stay on the coast 'till they Rotted.' The tars [sailors] considered their plight to be one of 'bondage,' in which they endured 'Barbarous & Unhumane Usage from their Commander.'"

Historians sometimes have difficulty determining whether it was the unruly actions of seamen or the extreme reactions of brutal captains that provoked mutinies. The trial transcript of *James Littman v. Peter Bostock,* which was heard in the Vice Admirality Court located in Charleston, South Carolina, gives a detailed picture of an incident aboard the *Prince George,* anchored along the Gambia River, in January 1753. In this instance, seaman James Littman accused Captain Peter Bostock of assault. Bostock countered that it was Littman's own violent behavior that necessitated stern discipline. "Defendant [Captain Peter Bostock] saith that the said James Littman at several other times and places was very often drunk and . . . very abusive to this Defendant and to the rest of the Officers . . . and without any thing being done or said to him . . . did make a great riot and noise on board the said ship and cried out murder several times and behaved himself in a very disorderly and mutinous manner. Therefore this Defendant did for the Causes aforesaid put Irons upon and confined the said James Littman for about the space of twelve Hours. . . . What [Captain Bostock] so did was through Necessity and to keep James Littman, who was then running about the said Ship raving like a Madman, quiet and prevent him from raising a mutiny on Board."

strengthen the slaves's resolve. Risking shark infested waters in a desperate attempt to reach land required a measure of courage that sustained itself and grew over time. As historian Jay Coughtry explains: "Ordinary merchandise rotted, leaked, or became waterlogged. Slaves posed the added burden of being unwilling and, at times, uncooperative passengers: elaborate security measures were necessary in order to keep them from sabotaging the ship, jumping overboard, or elminating their captors altogether."[138] As fear of rebellion among slavers caused them to increase their crews, so did the captives' determination to fight against the unspeakable horrors of the Middle Passage.

Selling the Slave Cargo

When signs of land appeared, crew and captives began to realize that the agony of the Middle Passage was at an end. Seeing the land rise over the horizon meant, in the words of Thomas Howard, that "the traumatic middle passage, of months aboard ship, crowded, jostled, thirsting and weakened by disease [were ending]. The slave's chains hung heavier with each passing day, and the thought of relief from the dreadful rolling sea was revived by the sight of the green . . . [islands. Passengers were] anxious to swap the ship for anything on land, no matter if [they] knew nothing of where [they] were] or what [their] future held."[139]

As the ship neared port, the crew excitedly furled the sails and lowered the anchor. For many slaves, like Olaudah Equiano, the relief and happiness of the whites on board bewildered them. "At last we came in sight of the island of Barbados, at which the whites on board gave a great shout, and made many signs of joy to us," remembered Equiano. "We did not know what to think of this; but as the vessel drew nearer, we plainly saw the harbour, and other ships of different kinds and sizes."[140]

The arrival of a slaver generally caused a great stir and bustle. The captain or commanding officer ordered the gunner to fire a round on the ship's arrival. The gun fire attracted the attention of a harbor pilot, who helped the ship navigate its way into the port. The pilot also ferried a doctor out to the ship, who made sure the crew and captives were free of contagious diseases such as smallpox. Some accounts describe the vile smell of vomit, sweat, stale urine, and feces that came from the slave ship and wafted over the port when it arrived.

Registering the Goods and Inspecting the Cargo

Upon arrival, captains first had to register their merchandise. Government administrators, including the treasurer of the port, a court-appointed magistrate, a tax collector, and their guards and clerks, might assemble to evaluate the monetary value of the slaves. Either before the slaves disembarked or after they were brought to holding pens on land, the director and treasurer assembled the naked slaves and registered them on a sort of inventory list. Inspectors then carefully examined each slave by squeezing his or her limbs and body. Slaves showed their teeth, extended their arms, and flexed their muscles. Strong young male and female slaves commanded a high price, which officials marked on a piece of parchment and hung, like a price tag, around the slaves' necks. Then government officials divided the priced slaves into lots to decide how much import tax the captain and traders had to pay on the cargo.

Once the slaves had been registered and inspected, traders and seamen then herded them into holding pens, or slave houses, which were long wooden or brick one-story houses, where they were, as Olaudah Equiano described, "all pent up together, like so many sheep in a fold, without regard to sex or age."[141]

Depending on the customs of the slave port, slaves who were sick or unhealthy were treated in various ways. In Charleston, South Carolina, a major slave port in the United States, officials insisted on examining all cargoes they suspected of carrying disease. According to Hugh Thomas, "Rather than land their cargoes directly in the city, slave traders unloaded their slaves on Sullivan's Island, off the coast of Charleston."[142] In this case, both crew and slaves lived in pest houses—rough wooden shacks—for ten days waiting for clearance. If anyone turned out to be suffering from smallpox, he or she had to stay there, quarantined for at least a month. In Cartagena de Indias, a slave port in Brazil, sick slaves were quarantined in barracoons, similar to the prisons the captives lived in on the African coast before they were shipped to the Americas.

Refuse Slaves

Generally, the captain first tried to sell his refuse slaves, those who were weak or had

A map from about 1657 depicts the West Indies island of Barbados, one of the ports where slave ships stopped after the Middle Passage.

The Crew at Port

Even as the surviving crew was about to sail home, officers often tried to abuse seamen and cheat them out of their yearlong wages. Captains sometimes purposely mistreated the sailors, hoping they would desert the ship so investors would not have to pay them the money they were owed. Other times, captains sailed without notice, leaving half of their men behind. In *Black Cargoes,* Daniel P. Mannix and Malcolm Cowley quote the testimony one witness gave to Parliament: "It was no uncommon thing for the captains to send on shore, a few hours before they sail, their lame, emaciated, and sick seamen, leaving them to perish."

been maimed or seriously harmed during the Middle Passage. To make the slaves more appealing, he attempted to hide the presence of physical weakness or diseases such as skin ailments or the bloody flux. For example, ship surgeons applied a mixture of iron rust and gun powder to hide the red sores of the slaves suffering from the skin disease, yaws.

Refuse slaves were taken ashore to a tavern and auctioned off "by inch of candle," meaning the auctioneer lit a candle and bidding for the refuse began. When one inch of the candle had burned, the bidding was closed and these slaves went to the highest bidders.

The price for a refuse slave was usually about half of what a healthy man or woman would bring. Sometimes it was as little as five or six dollars a head. "I was informed by a mulatto woman," Alexander Falconbridge said, "that she purchased a sick slave at Granada, upon speculation, for the small sum of one dollar, as the poor wretch was apparently dying of the flux."[143]

In 1756 Henry Laurens wrote to Samuel and William Vernon, his partners in Newport, Rhode Island, about a sale that did not go well:

We had as many purchasers as we could have wished for . . . but . . . many of them became extremely angry that we should invite them down from eighty or ninety miles distance to look at a parcel of "refuse slaves". . . . We were willing to believe that Captain [Caleb] Godfrey obtained the best [slaves] he could but, really, they were a wretched cargo. . . . God knows what we shall do with those that remain, they are a most scabby flock. . . . Several extreme[ly] sore eyes, three very puny children and, add to this, the worst infirmity of all others with which six or eight are attended . . . old age.[144]

If they found no buyers at their first stop, ship captains traveled from port to port with their shipload of slaves. As one slave merchant wrote in a letter to his partner in 1750, "I am now to inform you (and with inexpressible grief) that I have a letter dated at Barbados advising that (the captain of our ship) was under sail for St. Kitts (there being no market for slaves at Barbados)."[145]

Sometimes slaves were in such bad shape that no one would buy them. In that case, traders simply turned the unwanted slaves loose on the wharves. Having neither food or water and no means of supporting themselves, the slaves usually died of starvation or thirst. James Morley, a gunner in the 1760s, recalled seeing such captives "lying about the beach at St. Kitts, in the market place, and in the different parts of the town, in a very bad condition, and apparently nobody to take care of them."[146]

Slaves to be quarantined are led to a barracoon, which was also a burial ground for slaves who died of disease or starvation after the voyage.

Healthy Slaves

Upon arrival at port, traders immediately began preparing healthy slaves for sale. They fed them, washed them, oiled their skin, and cut their hair. They gave them clothes to wear and exercised them everyday until the day of sale. According to Hugh Thomas, the slaves "would be assembled in a camp, where they would be fed, cleaned, and otherwise looked after, in such a way that they would lose all trace of the 'fatigues' of the journey."[147]

Different ports offered different accomodations. In Rio de Janeiro, for example, slaves might live on the ground floors of a slave merchant's shop, where they were shaved and fattened, their skin oiled and sometimes painted to give the illusion of good health. Sometimes these merchants prepared African foods

made with manioc and cornmeal to "make the slaves feel at home," says Thomas. "Some religious instruction might casually be available. Tobacco and snuff were sometimes given to slaves who behaved well. . . . Slaves would also be made to dance and sing, as they were required to do on board the slave ship."[148]

Some English trading companies performed elaborate preparations, especially if the slaves were to be resold in Spanish markets, such as those in South America. They bathed their slaves in water treated with herbs, gave them two meals a day, along with what slavers considered luxuries: a pipe full of tobacco to smoke and a swig or two of rum every day.

Preparing the slaves for market was less elaborate in other areas, however. In the West Indies, for instance, fattening a slave for sale occurred less frequently than it did in

Brazil. French slavers in Santo Domingo were primarily interested in selling their human cargo as quickly as possible, partly because they believed that it was less costly to replace slaves with new shipments than to spend time or money on their upkeep.

Advertising the Sale

The arrival of a cargo of slaves also meant alerting buyers. Sometimes slave traders made arrangements beforehand to supply slaves to a particular merchant or plantation owner. Other times, a slave trading firm sent broadsides or flyers to the country planters and ran advertisements of its newly arrived crop of slaves in the newspaper.

Slave merchants were rarely able to predict exactly how far in advance they would be able to announce a slave sale because it was hard to tell whether a new shipment of slaves would be healthy or require several days in quarantine. Even if the slaves did arrive in good health, organizers still needed time to get everything ready. For example, according to Hugh Thomas, "ten to twenty days were needed in Saint-Domingue to dispose of five to six hundred slaves."[149]

Newspapers regularly announced the arrival of slave cargoes in the "Shipping News" section, along with other imported items, including cloth, sugar, ivory, and rum. Merchants often supplemented these announcements with weekly ads listing the availability of all of their merchandise. Usually, though, slave trading firms like Austin and Laurens of Charleston, South Carolina, advertised a slave sale separately and included a specific date and location for the sale.

Typical advertisements that appeared in the *South Carolina Gazette* read, "To be Sold on Thursday next, being the 5th of October, by George Austen for ready Money, a Choice Parcel of Negroes, lately imported in the ship Edward to be seen on Board the said Ship at Eliots Wharff."[150] Another boasted, "Just Imported in the Snow Fortune, Edward Boucier Master about 180 Slaves, from the Windward and Gold-Coast directly, all in good Health. To be sold on Wednesday the 3d of July next to Austen and Laurens."[151]

Nearing Land

Sometimes, as historians Daniel P. Mannix and Malcolm Cowley attest in *Black Cargoes,* during the last few days of the voyage there was a sort of celebration, a costume party aboard ship. In his memoirs, Captain Theodore Canot describes the scene he witnessed several times aboard the slavers he commanded.

"The sight of land is commonly the signal for merriment, for a well-behaved cargo is invariably released from shackles, and allowed . . . on deck. The Tanks are thrown open for unrestricted use. 'The cat' is cast into the sea. Strict discipline is relaxed. . . . Sailors . . . share their biscuits and clothing with the blacks. The women, who are generally without garments, appear in costume from the wardrobes of tars [sailors], petty officers, mates, and even captains. Sheets, table-cloths, and spare sails, are torn to pieces for raiment [clothing], while shoes, boots, caps, oilcloths, and monkey jackets, contribute to the . . . masquerade."

Market Day

Early on, the primary slave buyer was the European planter, who bought slaves for his plantation in the West Indies, South America, or the southern United States. In Brazil and other parts of South America, mine owners also purchased slaves. However, by the end of the eighteenth century, the slave market had begun to attract people of more modest means, who wanted to buy a slave or two to increase their status as well as help with chores.

Often the buyer's home was many miles away from the port city, and wealthy planters might send their overseers to select the slaves. In the 1700s, it might take all day to travel the forty, sixty, or even eighty miles to auctions. And when slave buyers finally arrived at the port city, they wanted to bid on and purchase slaves as quickly as possible.

Their plantations needed the labor immediately, and to return empty-handed might mean losing out on a profitable harvest.

George Pinckard, a British surgeon, visited the West Indies at the end of the eighteenth century and described a slave sale he witnessed there. Pinckard compared the atmosphere of the sale to a public fair. He thought people treated it as a "festive day. . . . The belles and beaux appeared in their Sunday suits. Even the children were in full-dress, and their slaves decked out in holiday clothes. . . . To the inhabitants it seemed a day of feasting and hilarity."[152]

Yet Pinckard also recognized the disturbing contrast between the festive atmosphere and the horror and tragedy of the afternoon. He later wrote, "But to the poor Africans it was a period of heavy grief and affliction; for they were to be sold as beasts of burden—torn from each other."[153]

Europeans in the New World bought the newly arrived slaves to work on plantations, in mines, or as servants.

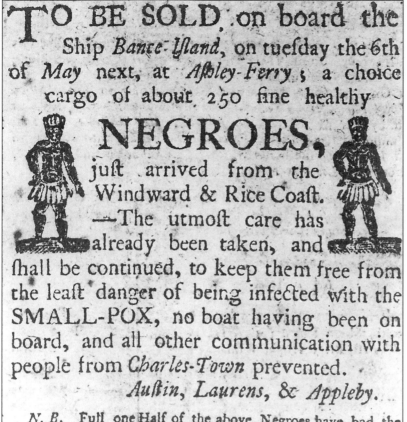

TO BE SOLD, on board the Ship *Bance-Island*, on tuesday the 6th of *May* next, at *Ashley-Ferry*; a choice cargo of about 250 fine healthy NEGROES, just arrived from the Windward & Rice Coast. —The utmost care has already been taken, and shall be continued, to keep them free from the least danger of being infected with the SMALL-POX, no boat having been on board, and all other communication with people from *Charles-Town* prevented.

Austin, Laurens, & Appleby.

N. B. Full one Half of the above Negroes have had the SMALL-POX in their own Country.

An advertisement describes a cargo of slaves for sale. Slaves were sold by auction, scramble, or private treaty.

The Method of Sale: Slave Auction

Merchants sold slaves either by public auctions, scrambles, or private treaties. The most common method was the auction. Frequently, they were held in the streets of a slave port, although they might be held in a large room or a tavern. In Charleston, Vendue Range, a short walk from the wharf where the slaves arrived, was a popular open-air meeting place for slave sales.

Before the auction, slave traders dressed the slaves. Usually the women wore blue flannel dresses, and the men wore blue cotton trousers. In the winter, sometimes slave traders gave the slaves warmer clothes and shoes to wear. At the auction, buyers inspected the slaves much in the same way that the ship's surgeons had done on the coast of Africa. According to George Pinckard,

> The slaves were brought in, one at a time, and placed . . . before the bidders, who handled and inspected them, with as little concern as if they had been examining cattle. . . . They turned them about, felt them, viewed their shapes and limbs, and looked into their mouths, made them jump and throw out their arms, and subjected them to all the means of trial as if dealing for a horse or other brute animal.[154]

The indifference and coldness of the slave buyer toward the enslaved African is reflected in the words of Bryan Edwards, a member of the Jamaica assembly and a planter and slave owner. In his history of the West Indies, published in 1794, Edwards talks about the misconceptions people have about slave auctions. His attitude was probably typical of most slave owners at the time, and it reveals how little they knew about the African captive about to be sold.

"Although there is something extremely shocking to the humane and cultivated mind in the idea of beholding a numerous body of our unfortunate fellow creatures in captivity and exile, exposed naked to public view, and sold like a herd of cattle, yet I could never perceive that the Negroes themselves were oppressed with many of those painful sensations which a person unaccustomed to the scene would naturally attribute to such apparently wretchedness. . . . They commonly express great eagerness to be sold, presenting themselves with cheerfulness and alacrity for selection and appearing mortified and disappointed when refused."

Often buyers required the slaves to remove their clothing to examine them, making sure they were healthy and fit.

The Methods of Sale: Scrambles

Healthy slaves were ordinarily sold at scrambles. A scramble sale was held either on board a ship or in a merchant's yard. Before the scramble began, the merchant or slave ship captain assigned a price to each slave, and buyers agreed to pay the price. The merchant or captain then gave a signal, perhaps a drum beat, and the scramble began. At that moment, according to ship surgeon Alexander Falconbridge,

the doors of the yard were suddenly thrown open and in rushed a considerable number of purchasers, with all the ferocity of brutes. Some instantly seized such of the Negroes as they could conveniently lay hold of with their hands. Others being prepared with several handkerchiefs tied together, encircled as many as they were able. While others, by means of a rope, effected the same purpose.[155]

During a scramble, the competition for particular slaves could also become violent. Sometimes fistfights broke out among buyers over especially desirable slaves. According to merchant Henry Laurens, "Some of the buyers went to collaring each other and would have come to blows had it not been prevented in contending [struggling] for their choice."[156]

In the meantime, the slaves were terrified. As Olaudah Equiano recalls,

We were not many days in the merchant's custody, before we were sold after their usual manner, which is this: On a signal given . . . the buyers rush at once into a yard where the slaves are confined, and make choice of that parcel they like best. The noise and clamor with which this is attended, and the eagerness visible in the countenances of the buyers, serve not a little to increase the apprehension of terrified Africans. . . . In this manner, without [hesitation], are relations and friends separated, most of them never to see each other again.[157]

Alexander Falconbridge, who witnessed a number of scrambles in the West Indies, also wrote about the slaves' fear during such sales:

It is scarcely possible to describe the confusion of which this mode of selling is productive. It likewise causes much animosity among the purchasers who not infrequently fall out and quarrel with each other. The poor astonished Negroes were so terrified by these proceedings, that several of them, through fear climbed over the walls of the courtyard and ran wild about the town, but were soon hunted down and retaken.[158]

The Methods of Sale: Private Treaties

Private treaties were the least common method of sale. However, they did happen from time to time. In the case of a treaty, a slave trader made an agreement ahead of time with a planter, group of planters, trading firm, or factor to buy the slaves he brought from Africa. In a sense, the promise to buy the slaves helped fund the voyage because investors knew they would have a ready market in the West Indies waiting for their shipment. As part of the treaty and to assure investors that they could count on making a certain amount of money, slave buyers agreed on a set price even before the voyage began. In the case of the private treaty, it was as if the ship and all its of crew members were sent to Africa to fill an order.

A dealer inspects a slave to determine his health and fitness at an auction in Virginia.

Completing the Triangle

After all of the slaves had been landed and sold, the captain and remaining crew loaded hogsheads of goods into the ship's empty hold. Stocked with these goods, the ship returned to its home port. Ships heading up the coast of North America to Rhode Island brought molasses that distilleries made into rum. Ships heading across the Atlantic Ocean carried cotton from South Carolina and rum and sugar from the West Indies. This final leg of the journey completed the transatlantic Triangle of Trade.

Families for Sale

During a slave sale, families were often separated. Most buyers bid for what they needed, not caring if they tore families apart. The anguish that loved ones expressed when they realized they would never see each other again was heartbreaking.

On one occasion, however, bidders did fight to keep families together. In his *Notes on the West Indies,* published in 1806, George Pinckard describes the near desperation of a husband who was about to be sold away from his wife. The slave, newly arrived from Africa, spoke only his native language and had to communicate his terror through hand signals.

"A tall and robust Negro, on being brought into the auction room, approached the table with a fine Negress hanging upon his arm. The man was ordered to mount [the auction block]. He obeyed, though manifestly with reluctance . . . grief was in his eye. . . . Then looking at the woman, he made signs expressive of great distress. Next, he pointed to her, and then to the chair. . . . He looked again at the woman, again pointed to the chair, held up two fingers to the auctioneer, and implored the multitude in anxious suppliant gestures. . . . [Finally] a second chair was brought and the woman was placed at the side of her husband . . . (who) hung upon the neck of his wife, and embraced her with rapture. . . . The bidding was renewed."

The buyers eventually agreed to bid on both husband and wife.

Many slaves suffered painful separations from their families, and often never saw each other again.

Life aboard the ships that brought Africans to the Americas and European goods to Africa was a grueling and murderous experience. For the Africans, forced to wear shackles and imprisoned in stifling slave holds, daily life aboard a slave ship was horrendous. For crew members, it was also miserable, filled with abuse, incurable disease, and continual fear and violence. Only for investors, who generally never made the trip, was there any benefit at all.

As devastating as life on an African slave ship was, it is still a significant part of human history. Surviving everyday life aboard a slaver was a remarkable feat. Endurance is a victory and should be celebrated. So should those who resisted, rebelling against the tyranny of brutal treatment and loss of freedom, fighting to reclaim liberty. Life on an African slave ship is a piece of our past we will never repeat, but it is also a piece we must never forget.

After the Slave Trade

Even after the auctions and sales were complete, the journey for the slaves was not over. Led away from their families, they traveled again, this time to the homes of their masters, perhaps located in the heart of a city like Charleston or in the country on a plantation. For some, this journey would be the last. For others, it was simply a prelude of more to come.

The slaves traveled by cart, foot, and horse en route to their new homes. Writer Julius Lester explains that,

> Once sold to a trader, the slaves were chained together and marched away, sleeping in the woods and fields at night, until they reached their destination some weeks later. Once there, the slave trader rested them for a few days, gave them new clothing, and sold them to new masters who would march them to the plantations. These would be their "homes" until they were sold again, escaped, or died.[159]

Between 1440 and 1870, more than 4 million Africans were delivered this way to Brazil, where they worked in mines and on coffee plantations. Another 4 million arrived in the West Indies to farm sugar plantations. Many of those men, women, and children spent a few years in the Caribbean, becoming what slave traders called "seasoned." After learning the ways of slave life in the New World, seasoned slaves, nearly 500,000, were sold to plantation owners in the United States.

Factors Contributing Toward Abolition

During the seventeenth and eighteenth centuries, however, just as slave trading reached its height, things began to change. People in Europe and the United States started challenging both the business and the philosophy of enslaving human beings. In England, social reformer Thomas Clarkson made abolishing the slave trade his lifelong work. He teamed up with William Wilberforce, a brilliant orator and member of the British parliament, and for more than twenty years, they battled in Parliament to gain support for their movement.

Meanwhile, across the ocean in America, colonists in Rhode Island passed a law in 1652 that freed adult slaves after ten years. All enslaved children were freed when they turned twenty-four years old. In Pennsylvania, Quakers led the antislavery, or abolitionist, movement, joining forces with such colonial leaders as Benjamin Franklin and Benjamin Rush, both staunch opponents of slavery.

Thomas Paine was another very vocal American reformer who spoke out against the horrors of the slave trade. Paine argued that the United States of America had been established to represent the ideals of a republic, which championed liberty and human dignity; such a country could not also tolerate the dehumanizing tyranny of slavery.

Those most closely involved in the slave trade knew its horrors all too well. Among the many abolitionists who gave vivid descriptions of slavery and the slave trade, none were more powerful than those of the slave ship captains and seamen who served in the trade for years. "[This profession] brings a numbness upon the heart and renders those who are engaged in it too indifferent to the sufferings of their fellow creatures,"[160] declared John Newton before a Parliamentary hearing. During similar proceedings, yet another captain proclaimed, "The African trade is a national sin."[161]

Ultimately, European and American abolitionists convinced government officials that the buying and selling of people had to end. After much debate, on March 12, 1807, England's Parliament passed a bill outlawing the slave trade. A few months later, the U.S. Congress also passed legislation that made the trade illegal. It was no longer legal to transport slaves from Africa to America, but slavery itself lasted for another half century in the United States.

At the same time, an illegal slave trade developed. Smugglers carried on a brisk and profitable business. During this time, England, the nation that spearheaded the trade in the seventeenth and eighteenth centuries, took responsibility for policing the Atlantic, capturing illegal slaving ships, and freeing the Africans on board.

After an agonizing journey from Africa, slaves were usually sold into a life of grueling plantation work.

The Economic Effects

Some historians believe that changing philosophical and religious convictions led to the success of the abolitionist movement. Others point to the political unrest that occurred at the end of the eighteenth century. The French and American revolutions may have inspired an increased number of slave revolts, especially in the Caribbean, and some historians maintain that these violent uprisings contributed to the growing resistance to and eventual defeat of the slave trade.

A third school of thought contends, though, that the trade simply no longer met the needs of a changing economic system.

During the eighteenth century, the slave trade supported the early forms of a capitalist structure. At that time, the New World's need for cheap labor made the African slave trade a profitable venture.

However, by the beginning of the nineteenth century, as the most powerful nations began to rely heavily on industry, slave labor started to lose its value. In its place, the working-class wage earner became the more profitable investment for capitalists who had, at first, poured all of their resources into supplying planters with slaves. These capitalists turned their attention to factories and mills, investing heavily in the skilled and unskilled workers who worked for a fraction of what it cost to import slave labor from Africa.

Statesman and inventor Benjamin Franklin urged the newly formed U.S. government to abolish slavery.

President Abraham Lincoln (third from left) at the signing of the Emancipation Proclamation, the amendment that abolished slavery.

Finally, an End

Whether for philosophical or economic reasons, by the early nineteenth century, abolitionists in the United States were gaining ground. Although it took nearly sixty years, slavery was finally abolished with Abraham Lincoln's Emancipation Proclamation. During those years, the drive to reform society, together with shifting economic needs, pointed the United States toward a new vision that viewed slavery as unnecessary and unacceptable. But, as historian Edward Reynolds asserts, "the interest in reform . . . was not a concern for slaves as such. Nor was the fight for abolition and emancipation an admission that black people were equal to whites."[162]

In fact, historians maintain that as notions of emancipation took hold, white supremacy and racism increased. Those attitudes grew in intensity, becoming a fixed part of American Society. Yet, despite those attitudes, former slaves and the generations that followed prevailed and carved out lives for themselves.

On Sullivan's Island, a small island off the coast of Charleston, South Carolina, that once served as the port of entry for at least a third of the slaves who arrived in the United States, there stands a plaque, commemorating the strength and determination of the captured Africans. The plaque reads,

WE COMMEMORATE THIS SITE AS THE ENTRY OF AFRICANS WHO CAME AND WHO CONTRIBUTED TO THE GREATNESS OF OUR COUNTRY. THE AFRICANS WHO ENTERED THROUGH THIS PORT HAVE MOVED ON TO MEET THE CHALLENGES CREATED BY INJUSTICES, RACIAL AND ECONOMIC DISCRIMINATIONS, AND WITHHELD OPPORTUNITIES. AFRICANS AND AFRICAN AMERICANS THROUGH THE SWEAT OF THEIR BROW, HAVE DISTINGUISHED THEMSELVES IN THE ARTS, EDUCATION, MEDICINE, POLITICS, LAW, ATHLETICS, RESEARCH, BUSINESS, INDUSTRY, ECONOMICS, SCIENCE, TECHNOLOGY, AND COMMUNITY AND SOCIAL SERVICES.

THIS MEMORIAL . . . SERVES AS A REMINDER OF A PEOPLE WHO—DESPITE INJUSTICE AND INTOLERANCE—PAST AND PRESENT, HAVE RETAINED THE UNIQUE VALUES, STRENGTHS AND POTENTIAL THAT FLOW FROM OUR WEST AFRICAN CULTURE WHICH CAME TO THIS NATION THROUGH THE MIDDLE PASSAGE.[163]

Notes

Introduction: Voyage of Cruelty

1. John Henrik Clarke, introduction to *The Middle Passage*, by Tom Feelings. New York: Dial, 1995, n.p.
2. Quoted in Hugh Thomas, *The Slave Trade*. New York: Simon & Schuster, 1997, p. 415.
3. Quoted in Thomas, *The Slave Trade*, p. 413.
4. Quoted in Thomas, *The Slave Trade*, p. 418.
5. Clarke, in Feelings, *The Middle Passage*, n.p.
6. Clarke, in Feelings, *The Middle Passage*, n.p.
7. Clarke, in Feelings, *The Middle Passage*, n.p.
8. Daniel P. Mannix, in collaboration with Malcolm Cowley, *Black Cargoes*. New York: Viking, 1962, p. 141.
9. Clarke, in Feelings, *The Middle Passage*, n.p.
10. Clarke, in Feelings, *The Middle Passage*, n.p.
11. Clarke, in Feelings, *The Middle Passage*, n.p.

Chapter 1: The History of the Slave Trade

12. Olaudah Equiano, *The Interesting Narrative of the Life of Olaudah Equiano*. Boston: Bedford Books, 1995, p. 47.
13. Equiano, *The Interesting Narrative of the Life of Olaudah Equiano*, p. 47.
14. Equiano, *The Interesting Narrative of the Life of Olaudah Equiano*, p. 53.
15. Quoted in Thomas, *The Slave Trade*, p. 25

16. John Hope Franklin and Alfred A. Moss Jr., *From Slavery to Freedom*, 7th ed. New York: McGraw-Hill, 1994, p. 27.
17. Eric R. Wolf, *Europe and the People Without History*. Berkeley and Los Angeles: University of California Press, 1982, p. 129.
18. James Pope-Hennessey, *Sins of the Fathers: A Study of the Atlantic Slave Traders, 1441–1807*. New York: Capricorn Books, 1967, p. 12.
19. Donald R. Wright, *African Americans in the Colonial Era: From African Origins Through the American Revolution*. Arlington Heights, IL: Harlan Davidson, 1990, p. 46.
20. Thomas, *The Slave Trade*, pp. 262–64.
21. Quoted in Edward Reynolds, *Stand the Storm*. London: Allison & Burby, 1985, p. 101.
22. Pope-Hennessey, *Sins of the Fathers*, p. 13.
23. Pope-Hennessey, *Sins of the Fathers*, p. 13.
24. Pope-Hennessey, *Sins of the Fathers*, p. 15.
25. Pope-Hennessey, *Sins of the Fathers*, p. 17.
26. Pope-Hennessey, *Sins of the Fathers*, p. 19.

Chapter 2: The Journey to Africa

27. Quoted in Pope-Hennessey, *Sins of the Fathers*, pp. 18–19.
28. Quoted in Thomas Howard, ed., *Black Voyage*. Boston: Little, Brown, 1971, p. 204.
29. Quoted in David Northrup, ed., *The At-*

lantic Slave Trade. Lexington, MA: D. C. Heath, 1994, p. 84.

30. Quoted in Howard, *Black Voyage*, p. 87.
31. Quoted in Howard, *Black Voyage*, p. 56.
32. Quoted in Marcus Rediker, *Between the Devil and Deep Blue Sea: Merchant, Seamen, Pirates and the Anglo-American Maritime World, 1700–1750*. Cambridge, England: Cambridge University Press, 1987, pp. 116–17.
33. Quoted in Reynolds, *Stand the Storm*, p. 30.
34. Mannix and Cowley, *Black Cargoes*, p. 142.
35. Rediker, *Between the Devil and Deep Blue Sea*, p. 84.
36. Richard H. Dana Jr., *Two Years Before the Mast*. New York: Dodd, Mead, 1946, p. 9.
37. Rediker, *Between the Devil and the Deep Blue Sea*, p. 84.
38. Rediker, *Between the Devil and the Deep Blue Sea*, p. 84.
39. Dana, *Two Years Before the Mast*, p. 9.
40. W. Jeffrey Bolster, *Black Jacks: African Seamen in the Age of Sail*. Cambridge, MA: Harvard University Press, 1997, p. 79.
41. Bolster, *Black Jacks*, p. 79.
42. Mannix and Cowley, *Black Cargoes*, p. 143.
43. Quoted in Mannix and Cowley, *Black Cargoes*, p. 143.
44. Michael H. Cottman, *The Wreck of the "Henrietta Marie."* New York: Harmony Books, 1999, p. 46.
45. Quoted in Elizabeth Donnan, *Documents Illustrative of the History of the Slave Trade to America*, vol. I. Washington, DC: Carnegie Institute of Washington, 1935, p. 459.

Chapter 3: Capturing the Slaves

46. Ottabah Cugoano, *Narrative of the Enslavement of Ottobah Cugoano, a Native African; published by himself in the year 1787*. http://metalab.unc.edu/docsouth/neh/cugoano/cugoano.html, p. 123–24.
47. Cugoano, *Narrative of the Enslavement . . .*, p. 124.
48. Cugoano, *Narrative of the Enslavement . . .*, p. 124.
49. Quoted in Howard, *Black Voyage*, p. 117.
50. Quoted in Howard, *Black Voyage*, p. 117.
51. Quoted in Howard, *Black Voyage*, p. 37.
52. Quoted in Howard, *Black Voyage*, pp. 38–39.
53. Quoted in Reynolds, *Stand the Storm*, p. 40.
54. Quoted in Reynolds, *Stand the Storm*, p. 40.
55. Quoted in Reynolds, *Stand the Storm*, p. 34.
56. Quoted in Reynolds, *Stand the Storm*, p. 34.
57. Equiano, *The Interesting Narrative of the Life of Olaudah Equiano*, p. 47.
58. Quoted in Pope-Hennessey, *Sins of the Fathers*, p. 195.
59. Quoted in Reynolds, *Stand the Storm*, p. 40.
60. Quoted in Reynolds, *Stand the Storm*, p. 45.
61. Quoted in Bolster, *Black Jacks*, p. 48.
62. Bolster, *Black Jacks*, p. 56.
63. Quoted in Bolster, *Black Jacks*, p. 56.
64. Quoted in Howard, *Black Voyage*, p. 82.
65. Quoted in Reynolds, *Stand the Storm*, p. 45.
66. Quoted in Howard, *Black Voyage*, p. 85.

Chapter 4: The Middle Passage

67. Equiano, *The Interesting Narrative of the Life of Olaudah Equiano*, p. 54.
68. Quoted in Howard, *Black Voyage*, p. 94.
69. Clarke in Feelings, *The Middle Passage*, n.p.
70. Clarke in Feelings, *The Middle Passage*, n.p.
71. Quoted in Howard, *Black Voyage*, p. 81.
72. Quoted in Thomas, *The Slave Trade*, p. 412.
73. Quoted in Julius Lester, *To Be a Slave*. New York: Dell, 1968, p. 24.
74. Quoted in Lester, *To Be a Slave*, p. 29.
75. Quoted in Pope-Hennessey, *Sins of the Fathers*, p. 3.
76. Quoted in Pope-Hennessey, *Sins of the Fathers*, p. 3.
77. Quoted in Howard, *Black Voyage*, p. 84.
78. Quoted in Thomas, *The Slave Trade*, p. 412.
79. Quoted in Howard, *Black Voyage*, p. 133.
80. Mannix and Cowley, *Black Cargoes*, p. 113.
81. Quoted in Howard, *Black Voyage*, p. 129.
82. Quoted in Mannix and Cowley, *Black Cargoes*, p. 114.
83. Quoted in Mannix and Cowley, *Black Cargoes*, p. 114.
84. Quoted in Pope-Hennessy, *Sins of the Fathers*, p. 4.
85. Bolster, *Black Jacks*, p. 79.
86. Quoted in Rediker, *Between the Devil and the Deep Blue Sea*, p. 164.
87. Quoted in Rediker, *Between the Devil and the Deep Blue Sea*, p. 153.
88. Rediker, *Between the Devil and the Deep Blue Sea*, p. 165.
89. Quoted in Pope-Hennessy, *Sins of the Fathers*, p. 4.
90. Quoted in Howard, *Black Voyage*, p. 84.
91. Quoted in Henry Louis Gates Jr., ed., *The Classic Slave Narratives*. New York: Mentor/Penguin Books USA, 1987, p. 242.
92. Equiano, *The Interesting Narrative of the Life of Olaudah Equiano*, p. 54.

Chapter 5: Surviving the Journey

93. Cugoano, *Narrative of the Enslavement . . .*, pp. 124–25.
94. Quoted in Thomas, *The Slave Trade*, p. 311.
95. Equiano, *The Interesting Narrative of the Life of Olaudah Equiano*, p. 55.
96. Quoted in Reynolds, *Stand the Storm*, p. 51.
97. Quoted in Pope-Hennessey, *Sins of the Fathers*, p. 100.
98. Quoted in Mannix and Cowley, *Black Cargoes*, p. 114.
99. Quoted in Pope-Hennessey, *Sins of the Fathers*, p. 4.
100. Quoted in Michele Stepto, ed., *American Journey: The African-American Experience*. Woodbridge, CT: Primary Source Media, 1996, CD ROM.
101. Howard, *Black Voyage*, p. 90.
102. Quoted in Rediker, *Between the Devil and the Deep Blue Sea*, p. 93.
103. Rediker, *Between the Devil and the Deep Blue Sea*, pp. 92–93.
104. *South Carolina Gazette*, "Charles Town, October 3rd," October 3, 1754, p. 1.
105. *South Carolina Gazette*, "Charles Town, October 3rd," p. 1.
106. Quoted in Rediker, *Between the Devil and the Deep Blue Sea*, p. 94.
107. Quoted in Rediker, *Between the Devil and the Deep Blue Sea*, p. 93.
108. Equiano, *The Interesting Narrative of the Life of Olaudah Equiano*, p. 55.

109. Quoted in Rediker, *Between the Devil and the Deep Blue Sea*, p. 157.
110. Bolster, *Black Jacks*, p. 69.
111. Quoted in Bolster, *Black Jacks*, p. 3.
112. Equiano, *The Interesting Narrative of the Life of Olaudah Equiano*, p. 61.
113. Quoted in Rediker, *Between the Devil and the Deep Blue Sea*, pp. 1–2.
114. Quoted in Thomas, *The Slave Trade*, p. 428.
115. Thomas, *The Slave Trade*, p. 428.
116. Thomas, *The Slave Trade*, p. 428.
117. Howard, *Black Voyage*, p. 90.
118. Reynolds, *Stand the Storm*, p. 53.
119. Quoted in Brantz Mayer, *Captain Canot, an African Slaver*. New York: Arno, 1968, pp. 241–42.

Chapter 6: Resistance.
120. Cugoano, *Narrative of the Enslavement . . .*, p. 124.
121. Cugoano, *Narrative of the Enslavement . . .*, p. 124.
122. *South Carolina Gazette*, "Item," October 24, 1743, p. 1.
123. Quoted in Donnan, *Documents Illustrative of the History of the Slave Trade to America*, vol. 2. p. 265.
124. Quoted in Edward A. Pearson, *Designs Against Charleston: The Trial Record of the Denmark Vesey Slave Conspiracy of 1822*. Chapel Hill: University of North Carolina Press, p. 31.
125. Quoted in Thomas, *The Slave Trade*, p. 427.
126. Quoted in Thomas, *The Slave Trade*, p. 412.
127. Quoted in Mayer, *Captain Canot*, p. 103.
128. Quoted in Thomas, *The Slave Trade*, p. 426.
129. Quoted in Thomas, *The Slave Trade*, p. 427.
130. Quoted in Thomas, *The Slave Trade*, p. 427.
131. Jay Coughtry, *The Notorious Triangle: Rhode Island and the African Slave Trade, 1700–1807*. Philadelphia: Temple University Press, 1981, p. 152.
132. Quoted in Coughtry, *The Notorious Triangle*, p. 147.
133. Quoted in Coughtry, *The Notorious Triangle*, p. 150.
134. Quoted in Donnan, *Documents Illustrative of the History of the Slave Trade to America*, vol. 2, p. 462.
135. Quoted in Coughtry, *The Notorious Triangle*, p. 152.
136. Quoted in Coughtry, *The Notorious Triangle*, p. 158.
137. Quoted in Mayer, *Captain Canot*, p. 106.
138. Coughtry, *The Notorious Triangle*, p. 155.

Chapter 7: Selling the Slave Cargo
139. Howard, *Black Voyage*, p. 102.
140. Equiano, *The Interesting Narrative of the Life of Olaudah Equiano*, p. 57.
141. Equiano, *The Interesting Narrative of the Life of Olaudah Equiano*, p. 58.
142. Thomas, *The Slave Trade*, pp. 438–39.
143. Quoted in Mannix and Cowley, *Black Cargoes*, p. 128.
144. Quoted in Thomas, *The Slave Trade*, p. 439.
145. Quoted in Pope-Hennessey, *Sins of the Fathers*, p. 18.
146. Quoted in Thomas, *The Slave Trade*, p. 438.
147. Thomas, *The Slave Trade*, p. 432.
148. Thomas, *The Slave Trade*, p. 433.
149. Thomas, *The Slave Trade*, p. 437.
150. *South Carolina Gazette*, advertisement, September 30, 1732.
151. *South Carolina Gazette*, advertisement, June 20, 1754.

152. Quoted in Howard, *Black Voyage,* p. 112.
153. Quoted in Howard, *Black Voyage,* p. 112.
154. Quoted in Howard, *Black Voyage,* p. 112.
155. Quoted in Howard, *Black Voyage,* p. 137.
156. Quoted in Elizabeth Donnan, "Slave Trade into South Carolina before the Revolution," *American Historical Review,* July 1928, vol. 33, pp. 8–24.
157. Equiano, *The Interesting Narrative of the Life of Olaudah Equiano,* p. 58.
158. Quoted in Howard, *Black Voyage,* pp. 137–38.

Epilogue: After the Slave Trade

159. Lester, *To Be a Slave,* p. 52.
160. Quoted in Thomas, *The Slave Trade,* p. 311.
161. Quoted in Howard, *Black Voyage,* p. 145.
162. Reynolds, *Stand the Storm,* pp. 91–92.
163. Plaque, Sullivan's Island, Charleston, South Carolina, erected in 1999 by the South Carolina Department of Archives and History, The Charleston Club of South Carolina, and the Avery Research Center.

For Further Reading

Clifford Lindsay Alderman, *Rum, Slaves, and Molasses: The Story of New England's Triangular Trade.* New York: Crowell-Collier, 1972. Middle-grade level. A vivid account of the Triangle of Trade, tracing the route of an American slaver, the *Sukey,* as it sailed from New England to Africa to the Caribbean.

James Haskins and Kathleen Benson, *Bound for America: The Forced Migration of Africans to the New World.* New York: Lothrop, Lee & Shepard Books, 1999. Pictorially, this is an extraordinary book with highly evocative paintings. Concise, age-appropriate text gives movement and authenticity to the story of Africans who were captured, sold, and sent to the Americas as slaves.

Jim Haskins, *"Amazing Grace": The Story Behind the Song.* Brookfield, CT: Millbrook, 1992. "Amazing Grace" is among the most popular spirituals ever written. Through narration and clear full-color illustrations, this fluidly written book tells the story of the song's composer, John Newton, a reformed slave trader, and how he came to write the song and become a fervent abolitionist.

Suzanne Jurmain, *Freedom's Sons: The True Story of the Amistad Mutiny.* New York: Lothrop, Lee & Shepard Books, 1998. A well-written account of the slave mutiny aboard the *Amistad* slaver. Particularly vivid and appropriate for middle grades.

Colin A. Palmer, *The First Passage: Blacks in the Americas*, 1502–1617. New York: Oxford University Press, 1995. Well-organized, clearly written, with well-chosen photographs and illustrations included throughout, this young adult history gives an excellent description of the African cultures from which slaves came and, once here, the impact Africans Americans have had in shaping the country.

Velma Maia Thomas, *Lest We Forget: The Passage from African to Slavery and Emancipation.* New York: Crown, 1997. Created by using photographs and documents from the Black Holocaust Exhibit, this three-dimensional interactive book is a highly original, engaging approach that brings the whole history to life. Thomas's succinct, vivid text combines scholarship with easy to follow narrative.

Karen Zeinert, *The Amistad Slave Revolt and American Abolition.* North Haven, CT: Linnet Books, 1997. A good choice for middle school because of its close attention to historical detail and its organization, especially subheadings, which makes complex legal proceedings and the trials' impact on the abolitionist movement easier for younger readers to grasp.

Works Consulted

Books

W. Jeffrey Bolster, *Black Jacks: African American Seamen in the Age of Sail.* Cambridge, MA, Harvard University Press, 1997. A thorough, riveting account of the history of black sailors. An excellent analysis of life at sea as a central component of African American identity. Bolster's own experience as a seamen gives a vivid realism to life aboard eighteenth-century sailing ships.

Michael H. Cottman, *The Wreck of the "Henrietta Marie."* New York: Harmony Books, 1999. Traces the slaving journey of the *Henrietta Marie* as well as Cottman's spiritual journey while traveling from England to Africa to the Caribbean. Moving prose integrates history with narrative as Cottman reveals his participation working as an underwater archaeologist to uncover the remains of the sunken slave ship.

Jay Coughtry, *The Notorious Triangle: Rhode Island and the African Slave Trade, 1700–1807.* Philadelphia: Temple University Press, 1981. A well-documented scholarly work, with emphasis on the slave trade originating in the northeast. Interesting information on slave ship rebellion and resistance.

Harold Courlander, *The African.* New York: Henry Holt, 1967. A classic and the inspiration for Alex Haley's *Roots.* Passages on the capture of slaves and the Middle Passage are particularly affecting.

Richard H. Dana Jr., *Two Years Before the Mast.* New York: Dodd, Mead, 1946. This book really gives the reader a sense of life on board a sailing ship. Written originally as a protest against the treatment of seamen, this highly detailed firsthand account chronicles the journey from Boston to San Francisco in the mid-nineteenth century.

David Brion Davis, *Slavery and Human Progress.* New York: Oxford University Press, 1984. A brilliant scholarly work, which discusses many aspects of slavery and emancipation. Of particular interest was Davis's discussion of the antithetical relationship between slavery and human progress, especially the periods throughout history when many thought slavery facilitated progress.

Elizabeth Donnan, *Documents Illustrative of the History of the Slave Trade to America.* 4 vols. Washington, DC: Carnegie Institute of Washington, 1935. An exhaustive collection of documents about slave trading, including letters, personal narratives, testimonies before Parliament during the abolition movement and accounting records from captains and slave traders in America and England during the seventeenth and eighteenth centuries. Superb source for primary sources.

David Eltis, *Economic Growth and the End of the Transatlantic Trade.* New York: Oxford University Press, 1987. A technical, detailed economic analysis of the transatlantic trade during the late 1700s and early 1800s. Statistics include the number of voyages, volume of sales, and economic trends. Includes useful conversion tables that help calculate equivalency rates of the English pound from the eighteenth century to the present.

Olaudah Equiano, *The Interesting Narrative of the Life of Olaudah Equiano*. Boston: Bedford Books, 1995. One of the most significant original documents from the era. This remarkable autobiography, written by a freed slave, chronicles how Equiano was captured, sold into slavery, freed, and extremely involved in the abolitionist movement. No other work surpasses this in documenting the experience from the slave's perspective.

Tom Feelings, *The Middle Passage*. New York: Dial, 1995. This is primarily a large-format visual book, with beautifully reproduced drawings by Tom Feelings. An especially powerful pictorial recounting of the Middle Passage, including an emotionally evocative text by historian John Henrik Clark.

John Hope Franklin and Alfred A. Moss Jr., *From Slavery to Freedom*. New York: McGraw-Hill, 1994. 7th ed. This authoritative history is an excellent resource for overview as well as specific information. Particularly useful were the history of slavery and the discussion of African slavery and colonization. Contains good full-color photographs and reproductions.

Thomas R. Frazier, ed., *Afro-American History: Primary Sources*. New York: Harcourt, Brace & World, 1970. The first chapter of this well-presented compendium of primary sources contains valuable material on various aspects of the slave trade, as related by African captives. Selections of the text might be used for student use as well.

Henry Louis Gates Jr., ed., *The Classic Slave Narratives*. New York: Mentor/Penguin Books USA, 1987. This record of original slave narratives is a rich resource material. Highly readable for middle-school students interested in using primary source material to gain further knowledge of slavery and the slave trade.

Graham Russell Hodges, ed., *Black Itinerants of the Gospel: The Narratives of John Jea and George White*. Madison, WI: Madison House, 1993. John Jea was an African captive who was freed but worked as a seamen aboard slave ships during the eighteenth century. He was also a minister, and his autobiography is a fascinating historical document, fusing political ideology with gospel. Includes a very informative introduction by Hodges.

Thomas Howard, ed., *Black Voyage*. Boston: Little, Brown, 1971. Among the most useful sources for this project. Incisive selections of primary sources that tell the story of the African slave trade from many different viewpoints, from slave to ship surgeon to captain to factor. Gives a whole picture by providing eyewitness detail of every aspect of the trade.

Charles Johnson, *Middle Passage*. New York: Plume/Penguin Books, 1990. A National Book Award winner, this spellbinding novel gives a feel for the slaving voyage in all its depravity. Although not appropriate for the student audience because of explicit sexual references and violence, it is wonderful background reading for adults interested in the subject.

Howard Jones, *Mutiny on the "Amistad."* Rev. Ed. New York: Oxford University Press, 1987. This thorough, highly readable narrative incorporates original material to give authenticity to this interesting portrait of Cinque as rebel leader.

Julius Lester, *To Be a Slave*. New York: Dell, 1968. Gripping, well-chosen firsthand accounts of enslaved Africans and African Americans. A history of slavery in America, from the Middle Passage to life on the plantation, told by the men, women, and children who lived through it.

Daniel P. Mannix, in Collaboration with Malcolm Cowley, *Black Cargoes*. New York: Viking, 1962. A good source for primary sources relating particularly to crew treatment, the role of the captain on board and in Africa, and the leaders behind the abolitionist movement. Includes an informative chapter on early American trade as well.

Brantz Mayer, *Captain Canot, an African Slaver*. New York: Arno, 1968. A vivid firsthand account of a slave trader during the mid-nineteenth century, when the African slave trade was illegal. Fascinating material, including detailed reporting on how the Africans were directly involved in the trade.

David Northrup, ed., *The Atlantic Slave Trade*. Lexington, MA: D. C. Heath, 1994. A collection of essays by noted historians as well as excerpts of original firsthand documents that give a good understanding of the slave trade. Particularly useful were discussions on the number of slaves who were transported, the effects of the slave trade on Africa, and the reasons behind the abolitionist movement.

James Pope-Hennessey, *Sins of the Fathers: A Study of the Atlantic Slave Traders, 1441–1807*. New York: Capricorn Books, 1967. An excellent integration of original material with narrative, giving a full account of the Atlantic slave trade. An interesting re-creation of life aboard ship, at a trading post in Africa, on plantations, and at the slave market. A good, concise social, political, and economic picture of the trade.

Marcus Rediker, *Between the Devil and the Deep Blue Sea: Merchant, Seamen, Pirates, and the Anglo-American Maritime World, 1700–1750*. Cambridge, England: Cambridge University Press, 1987. A fascinating analysis of seafaring life during the age of sail. Particularly useful is Rediker's discussion of the seaman—his identity and his relationship with his peers and superiors—and the culture he created on land and on board ship.

Edward Reynolds, *Stand the Storm*. London: Allison & Busby, 1985. Reynolds, a historian born in Ghana, provides a concisely written but thorough overview of the slave trade. A good use of primary source material and a well-developed global view of the trade as forged connections with Africa, Europe, and the Americas.

Dava Sobel, *Longitude: The True Story of a Lone Genius Who Solved the Greatest Scientific Problem of His Time*. New York: Penguin Books, 1995. Transatlantic trade gained greater momentum with the discovery of how to calculate longitude. Sobel reveals the remarkable story in a highly readable narrative. Tangential to the life on the slaver, itself, but central to growth of the trade.

Michele Stepto, ed., *American Journey: The African-American Experience*. Woodbridge, CT: Primary Source Media, 1996. CD ROM. An excellent source for primary material, including pictures and documents, including a cutaway diagram of a slave ship, excerpts from Equiano's autobiography and other slave narratives, and a 1642 "Contract for Negroes."

Hugh Thomas, *The Slave Trade*. New York: Simon & Schuster, 1997. A good resource for primary material that presents the breadth of this international trade. An exhaustive study, especially in depicting the Portuguese, Spanish, and English drive to establish and develop the profitable use of slaves in the New World.

Selena Axelrod Wisnes, *Letters on West Africa and the Slave Trade*. New York:

1992. An interesting collection of material. The narrative style makes information accessible and especially useful for obtaining original documents to share with middle-school students.

Eric R. Wolf, *Europe and the People Without History.* Berkeley and Los Angeles: University of California Press, 1982. Clearly organized and extremely comprehensible, this book provides an excellent resource for teachers who want to understand the slave trade within a broader European context.

Donald R. Wright, *African Americans in the Colonial Era: From African Origins Through the American Revolution.* Arlington Heights, IL: Harlan Davidson, 1990. A cogent analysis of how Africans became integrated within the fabric of colonial America. The first chapter provides a clear explanation of the relationship between the demand for labor in North America and Africa's response in supplying slaves to meet that need.

Periodicals

A. M. Rosenthal, "On My Mind: When Is It News?" *New York Times*, September 3, 1999.

South Carolina Gazette, advertisement, September 30, 1732.

———, advertisement, June 20, 1754.

———, "Item," October 24, 1743.

Harvey Wish, "American Slave Insurrections Before 1861." *The Journal of the American Negro*, July 1937.

Internet Sources

Ottobah Cugoano, *Narrative of the Enslavement of Ottobah Cugoano, a Native of Africa; published by himself in the year 1787.* http://metalab.unc.edu/docsouth/neh/Cugoano/Cugoano.html.

Other Sources

Michele Stepto, ed., *American Journey: The African-American Experience.* Woodbridge, CT: Primary Source Media, 1996, CD ROM.

Federal Admiralty Court Records, Province and State of South Carolina, 1716–1789. *James Littman v. Peter Bostock*, 1753. National Archives Microfilm Publications, roll 3, vol. 4.

Elizabeth Donnan, "Slave Trade into South Carolina before the Revolution," *American Historical Review*, July 1928, vol. 33, pp. 804–28.

Index

Picture Credits

Cover photo: Peter Newark's American Pictures
© Paul Almasy/Corbis, 59
© Tony Arruza/Corbis, 67
© Dave Bartruff/Corbis, 20
© Bettmann/Corbis, 24, 27, 51, 70
© Corbis, 45, 50, 73
Dover Publications, 17
©Lowell Georgia/Corbis, 77

© Historical Picture Archive/Corbis, 55
Library of Congress, 42, 87, 90, 94
© Buddy Mays/Corbis, 25, 29
North Wind Picture Archives, 8, 9, 23, 33, 40, 46, 48, 58, 61, 63, 64, 71, 84, 89, 93, 95
Prints Old & Rare, 13
© Stock Montage, 32, 35, 37, 76, 82
© Adam Woolfitt/Corbis, 69

About the Authors

Joseph Kleinman has taught history for over twenty years on the middle school level as well as in college and graduate school. He currently teaches at the Fieldston School and is on the faculty of Bank Street College of Education. He holds a master's degree in social work from Hunter College, a master's from Bank Street in education administration, and a master's of philosophy in history from the Graduate Center, City University of New York. Eileen Kurtis-Kleinman is a freelance writer with a master's degree in education from Bank Street College of Education. They live in New York City with their three children.